BARRON'S
BUSINESS KEYS

KEYS TO BUYING FORECLOSED AND BARGAIN HOMES

Third Edition

Jack P. Friedman, Ph.D., C.P.A., M.A.I.
Real Estate Consultant
Dallas, Texas

Jack C. Harris, Ph.D.
Real Estate Consultant
Crystal Beach, Florida

Skip Stearns
Real Estate Foreclosure Investor and Hotel Expert
Stratham, New Hampshire

BARRON'S

D0916777

Jack P. Friedman is a real estate consultant in Dallas, Texas. Jack C. Harris is a real estate consultant in Crystal Beach, Florida. Skip Stearns is a real estate foreclosure investor and hotel expert in Stratham, New Hampshire. Friedman and Harris are the authors of *Keys to Investing in Real Estate*, *Keys to Mortgage Financing and Refinancing*, and *Keys to Purchasing a Condo or Co-op*.

All inquiries should be addressed to:
Barron's Educational Series, Inc.
250 Wireless Boulevard
Hauppauge, New York 11788
www.barronseduc.com

Library of Congress Catalog Card No. 2007047492

ISBN-13: 978- 0-7641-3883-6
ISBN-10: 0-7641-3883-9

Library of Congress Cataloging-in-Publication Data
Friedman, Jack P.
    Keys to buying foreclosed and bargain homes / Jack P. Friedman, Jack C. Harris, Skip Stearns. — 3rd ed.
        p. cm. — (Barron's business keys)
    Includes index.
    ISBN-13: 978-0-7641-3883-6
    ISBN-10: 0-7641-3883-9
    1. House buying.   2. Foreclosure.   3. Real estate investment.   I. Harris, Jack C., 1945– II. Stearns, Skip.   III. Title.

    HD1390.5.H36 2008
    332.63'24—dc22

                                                                    2007047492

PRINTED IN THE UNITED STATES OF AMERICA
9 8 7 6 5 4 3 2 1

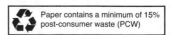 Paper contains a minimum of 15% post-consumer waste (PCW)

TABLE OF CONTENTS

IV. Buying a Handyman's Special

V. Buying at a Non-foreclosure Auction

VI. Negotiation and Buying Skills

1

GETTING A HOME FOR A BARGAIN

A home is probably the biggest investment you will make in your lifetime. If you can get a quality property that serves your purposes and save money in the process, you will reap important financial benefits.

Residential real estate is also an excellent vehicle for creating a real estate investment portfolio. In fact, many large fortunes owe their existence to timely acquisition of real estate and the ability to make those properties pay off. A big part of the success of getting a real estate portfolio off the ground is acquiring properties at below-market value prices.

In a home purchase, a bargain is one bought for less than its market value. However, a property's market value is not easy to determine because information about the market is incomplete and transactions are relatively infrequent. The lack of market information provides opportunities to buy below market value, but creates pitfalls as well. Sellers generally know what they own, including its problems. A property may be a bargain because an uninformed seller is asking too little, or is eager or desperate to sell. It may be a bargain because it was foreclosed and the lender/owner is under pressure to sell it quickly. In such cases, the more you know about market value, the better off you are.

It is possible to save a good deal of money in a home purchase in other ways as well. Unlike many things you buy, a home does not have an established, take-it-or-leave-it price. Even new homes are subject to negotiation between buyer and seller before a selling price is set. And there are several things that add up to that "price." A seller may agree to pay all or some of the items at closing that buyers normally pay, such as legal fees, appraisal fees, or discount points on a loan. There may be concessions in the contract that potentially add value to the home.

Seller financing may be part of the deal, the terms of which can be tailored to add value.

Obviously, understanding the bargaining process and what makes a property more valuable helps when you are trying to negotiate a favorable price. Even more important is how eager each party is to make a sale. In markets where there are many buyers and few homes available, the seller can hold out for top dollar. But in cases where buyers are hard to find and there are plenty of homes on the market, the buyer can bargain. When the seller is under pressure to move the property, the result is often termed a "distress sale." By finding and sizing up such sales, a homebuyer can save a great deal of money.

This book serves as a guide to finding and taking advantage of distress sale situations as well as other situations where there are opportunities to buy at below-market price or with favorable financing. In most cases, distress sales follow when the property owner is in financial trouble and must sell the property. Many of these homes become foreclosed. Then the home generally goes into an inventory of repossessed homes, which eventually become available for sale. Holders of these homes may offer attractive deals to prospective buyers. The book explains the foreclosure process and how you can bid on homes at a foreclosure sale. You will learn how to find and make offers on homes in danger of being foreclosed, often providing you a chance to help the homeowner and profit as well. Another section describes the types of holders of repossessed homes and how they go about liquidating these homes. Also included is a section on buying from these inventories. Many distressed properties are sold at auction, and a section details how a real estate auction works.

Distressed properties may appeal to homebuyers who thought they could never afford a home (there are some of these special programs for buyers with below-average incomes) and to real estate investors looking for good income-producing property. However, some of these properties are in poor condition or are located in areas that limit their value. This book will help you to evaluate an opportunity and to follow through once you decide on a course of action.

2

THE HOME-BUYING PROCESS

If you've never bought a home before, you may not be familiar with the steps required to make the purchase or even how to get started. Even if you already own a home, you may want to use this Key to review the general procedure.

Buying a home in a distress sale may be quite different from the typical purchase procedure. However, to appreciate how it differs, you should know the "normal" procedure. (Virtually every home purchase turns out to be an adventure and requires some extraordinary action by the buyer, seller, or both. Nevertheless, there is a sequence of steps that most buyers and sellers attempt to follow.)

At some point in time, you come to the conclusion that your present housing is no longer satisfactory. You begin a search of the housing market to see what is available. This can be done in many ways. You may visit a **broker** and inspect the homes currently listed for sale. Most brokers are members of **Multiple Listing Services**, which means they can show you most of the homes currently for sale in the area. In addition, you can check ads in the paper or watch for "For Sale" signs in the neighborhoods that most appeal to you. Many homeowners sell their homes without broker assistance. Such homes should be considered by the bargain-conscious buyer. Homebuilders may conduct **open houses** and employ a sales staff to show you their subdivisions. You may access the Web site of a real estate broker or local multiple-list association, as well as "For Sale by Owner" Web sites, to see what is on the market.

After making a preliminary search, you begin to form an idea of which areas, or specific homes, you like as well as how much house you can afford to buy. This latter point is important, since it makes no sense to consider homes you can't afford. A broker can work with you to determine your borrowing limit, or you can

3

visit a mortgage lender for the same purpose. The amount of loan you can get and how much it costs are determined by your income, credit history, and any long-term debts you now have. This process is known as *prequalifying* for a loan amount. You can take that one step further to gain pre-approval for an amount. This is the best way to be attractive to the seller, especially when you are competing with other interested buyers.

Once you have decided on a specific home, you begin the negotiation process with the owner. Generally, this begins when you make an offer to buy the home for a certain price. In the purchase of real estate, oral offers are worthless. To make a serious offer, you submit it using a form called a **binder** or **sales contract** and include a cash deposit (called *earnest money*). If your offer is below the price listed by the seller, and it usually is, the seller is likely not to accept your offer but instead to return a **counteroffer**. This may continue until both sides are satisfied or negotiations break down. The contract describes the rights of both buyer and seller, so make sure that everything you need is stated, including a **closing date** at which time the property will be transferred.

After the contract is signed, you need to arrange financing. Approval usually takes from two to eight weeks, depending on the type of financing sought. You should have included a **contingency** in the sales contract so that if the financing you need cannot be arranged, the sale is called off and you can reclaim the earnest money. With a signed sales contract, you can make a formal application for a loan from a lending institution or mortgage banker. Some sales are made without such financing when the buyer **assumes** the existing loan or the **seller** provides the **financing**. The lender must determine the value of the property by hiring an appraiser and **approve** the buyer for the amount of loan applied for. If the buyer is approved, the lender forwards the required money to the closing, where it is distributed to the seller, with set amounts going to other parties who are to receive a fee.

At the closing, all money is exchanged and title to the property changes hands. Generally, a **title insurance company** is involved to assure that the buyer is receiving secure legal title to the property. There are various expenses, such as legal fees or real estate taxes, imposed upon either or both parties to the sale that are paid at closing. Large expenses that sellers customarily pay for include the brokerage commission, title insurance, and legal fees. Sellers often agree to pay discount points on the buyer's loan. Buyers incur costs for insurance and tax escrows and prorations, appraisal, survey, credit check, mortgage insurance, and recording fees. The closing marks the end of the home-buying process.

3

WHAT IS MARKET VALUE?

There is a concept in economics called *market value*. It is a theoretical concept based on having a large number of buyers and sellers competing with one another. The buyer willing to pay the highest price and the seller willing to accept the lowest price strike a deal. Other buyers aren't willing to pay so much or owners to accept so little at that moment. Also, the products are all the same (a bushel of wheat, for example), and the buyers and sellers are both informed and knowledgeable.

The real estate market doesn't work that efficiently. Each property is unique. Buyers and sellers don't get together in a central location such as a stock or commodities market. It may take months or years of exposure to the market before a property fetches market value.

Market value is commonly applied in most real estate transactions. The definition used is as follows:

The most probable price that a property should bring in a competitive and open market under all conditions requisite to a fair sale, the buyer and seller each acting prudently and knowledgeably, and assuming the price is not affected by undue stimulus. Implicit in this definition is the consummation of a sale as of a specified date and the passing of title from seller to buyer under conditions whereby

- buyer and seller are typically motivated;
- both parties are well informed or well advised, and acting in what they consider their best interests;
- a reasonable time is allowed for exposure in the open market;
- payment is made in terms of cash in U.S. dollars or in terms of financial arrangements comparable thereto; and
- the price represents the normal consideration for the prop-

erty sold unaffected by special or creative financing or sales concessions granted by anyone associated with the sale.

Other definitions of *value* were introduced as a result of the savings and loan debacle of the late 1980s, which also introduced state certification and licensing of appraisers.

A real estate salesperson or broker is not a qualified appraiser. Brokers and salespeople may offer a comparative market analysis (CMA) or broker's opinion of value (BOV), but, in many transactions, neither of these is an acceptable substitute for an appraisal.

Where licensed salespeople or brokers stand to gain a large commission from a sale, and they are also asked their opinion of value, they may be apt to offer an opinion that they think will result in a sale or gain them the listing.

Certified or licensed appraisers are more independent of the transaction, and their appraisals are professionally derived. However, their opinions are still just opinions, carrying no guarantee.

Please see Key 58 for an explanation of appraisals to derive market value.

4

CAN YOU GET A BARGAIN HOME?

To get a bargain, you must be willing to spend the time and effort to become familiar with the market and investigate the property. Most people seeking foreclosed or distress sale property are hoping to get a good property at a steal. Some buyers indeed get exceptional values, taking advantage of situations that favor buyers and being in the right place at the right time. Others end up with properties that have more problems than expected, and eventually require so much additional investment that they, too, lose the homes to foreclosure. Then there are those who lose sight of why they are trying to buy a foreclosed home and pay too high a price in the competition to win the bidding.

The key to getting a bargain is knowing what you are getting and understanding what its value is in the market. Making "lowball" bids on any property available will probably not be successful. When it does work, you may be getting a property with so many problems that no other bidder was interested.

Most properties are offered "as is," but you may have the opportunity to inspect the property before making a bid. You should always take advantage of this opportunity when it is available, even to the extent of hiring a professional inspector for properties you are serious about. Further, do your homework. You should consider the neighborhood, especially how it influences the value of the property and how appropriate it is for the use you intend. If the property is surrounded by other vacant buildings, understand that you are gambling on recovery of the area at some time in the near future. Any risk that you are forced to take should be reflected in the price you offer.

You should always have a reference value to compare against the price you are prepared to pay for the property. The reference should be a comparable property in what you consider to be acceptable condition. You can estimate what it would take to make the property you are considering equal to the reference property. This amount should be deducted from the reference value when deciding on your "reservation price."

Your reservation price is the highest you should be willing to pay for the property. Consider the prices of other properties in the market, likely future opportunities to buy other properties, and how badly you want this one. Decide what price would be the most you would pay if you really had to. That amount is your reservation price. Write it on a piece of paper and do not allow yourself to pay more. You hope you can get the property for something less than your reservation price. If so, you may have gotten a true bargain. But never pay more than your reservation price even though it means not "winning" the bid.

You may even want to have an appraisal done on the property (see Key 58). This will tell you what comparable properties have sold for recently. The cost of the appraisal ($300–$500) can be worth it if it keeps you from making a costly error and paying too much for the property. Another approach is to include in the contract that the house must appraise for at least the amount you agree to pay. If it appraises for less than the contract, you can negotiate a lower price or walk away from the deal.

Holders of foreclosed homes are receiving little or no benefit from keeping the property in inventory. Therefore, they should be anxious to sell. However, they do want to get as high a price as possible. They may be willing to hold the property rather than sell it for less than they consider obtainable in the market. Sometimes you can get a bargain if you quickly satisfy what the holder needs. That may mean having the cash or prearranged financing to swing the deal. It may mean being able to complete the transaction without delay.

5

BUYING FOR RESALE OR INVESTMENT VERSUS HOMEOWNERSHIP

How you approach foreclosed real estate depends on whether you are looking for a property to live in or to rent out. To some extent, your situation will have a lot to do with whether you should consider distressed property at all.

When you buy a property to be your home, your primary concern is whether the property can provide the type of home environment you want. First, you want to locate in an area that is relatively convenient to your place of work and other areas you visit frequently. You want a neighborhood that is reasonably secure and a good place to raise a family or to do whatever your personal lifestyle entails. In general, an area where homeowners keep their properties in good order and where industrial, commercial, and heavy traffic is at a minimum helps protect the value of your investment. Finally, the home itself should be attractive and provide enough space for your needs.

For resale or investment property, your focus is different. If your intent is to resell soon after purchase, often called *flipping*, the price you pay must be significantly less than market value. You must buy the property at a price low enough that you can pay for necessary improvements to raise deficiencies to acceptable standards for resale, incur closing costs, holding costs, and resale expenses, and have enough left over for a profit. See Key 33 for tips on working up a bid.

If you want a property that can be rented for enough to cover expenses and provide some return, then you have other concerns. Only under special circumstances should you rely on appreciation in value to provide a return on your investment. The property should provide "cash flow"—that is, rental income must exceed out-of-pocket costs. Look for factors that might make it hard for you to keep the property rented. These include undesirable features that drive away tenants or cause a lot of turnover. For example, a high-crime area would repel good tenants and leave you with those to whom you might not want to rent. If the neighborhood is not well kept, the value of your property may decline unless the opportunity arises to convert to another use.

If you are buying a house that will be your home, you may be coming to the transaction with extra baggage. You may currently be obligated on a lease or own a home that must be sold before you can buy the new home. If this is the case, you may not be in a good position to bid for foreclosed property. Many sellers will not entertain offers contingent on the sale of other property. If you require approved financing, you face a handicap in competing with other buyers. Finally, many properties are offered "as is," and you may not be able to get a guarantee of good working order.

As an investor, on the other hand, you are probably in a better position to deal. However, you must still do your homework before negotiation and be ready to make a solid offer when an opportunity arises. You may even be able to identify several acceptable properties. Then you can go for the one that turns out to represent the best value. In that way, you will be less likely to overpay because you became wedded to one property.

A good approach to use as an investor is to determine whether the property will provide a cash flow. You can figure how much the monthly payments will be, and see whether rent will cover them. For example, suppose you will have the following monthly payments:

Principal and interest	$500.
Taxes	75.
Insurance	50.
Repairs, painting, maintenance	75.
Monthly requirements	$700.

If the property is not expected to rent for more than $700, you better pass it up because you will experience negative cash flow. Buy it only if it is likely to appreciate in value or provide other benefits in the future.

(For more on real estate investing, see Barron's *Keys to Investing in Real Estate*.)

6

PROFITING FROM FORECLOSURES AND BARGAIN HOMES

In making the simple assumption that there is an income opportunity in acquiring distressed real estate, a prospective homebuyer or investor has to consider his or her motives. Is there a short-term outlook, or is there a longer-term game plan? Is there an intermediate investment horizon that lies somewhere in between? Is the property intended for personal use?

As you will see elsewhere in this book, investors with a short-term strategy are often referred to as *flippers*. Before they purchase a property, they are already thinking about how to dispose of it, or "flip it," in the shortest possible time. These are investors driven by generating immediate return, which may or may not be invested in the next property. Some tax-savvy investors strategize to hold or possibly dwell in a property for the minimum period of time required to achieve favorable capital gains taxation. Because tax code changes from time to time, it is always recommended that you seek advice from your accountant or tax professional in this regard.

Assuming he or she has the tolerance and special knowledge or resources required to act as a landlord, the intermediate-term investor may rent the property, adding potential cash flow to the overall investment plan. When market conditions allow, some investors gravitate to the intermediate-term strategy to capitalize on rapid price growth. Those who plan to hold the acquired property for a longer period may be hoping to benefit from lower taxation upon resale, but they can profit additionally from rental income and market appreciation. Even under circumstances where rental income is just meeting or barely exceeding ongoing expenses, the long-term investor eyes long-term appreciation.

Both intermediate and long-term investors may claim depreciation expense on rental property, a noncash tax deduction on their income tax returns. Because the tax benefit of accumulated depreciation may be taxed upon resale, professional tax planning is advised.

Regardless of how long you expect to hold foreclosed or bargain property, the purchase price is the most critical element to successful ownership. Knowing the real estate market and buying property under favorable circumstances will set the tone for each investment you make. How well you buy may determine how long you choose to hold the asset. There are four components to be considered in the investment plan for any property:

1. Purchase price
2. Renovation expenses
3. Other expenses
4. Resale price

Purchase price is simple to consider but often the most challenging about which to feel confident. The question is, For how much below current conservative market value can the property be acquired? The starting point is knowing competitive market values, or having someone on your team, perhaps a real estate agent or appraiser, who can advise you. As the purchase price approaches the anticipated resale price, the deal becomes less attractive to the investment-driven buyer who may be calculating a minimum margin threshold. For some buyers who intend to live in the subject property, buying at any discount to market price may be the objective, because they are banking on long-term appreciation. Again, the most important thing is working toward the best achievable discount at the time of purchase. Conservative perspectives on both entry and exit pricing are encouraged. It is far better to be pleasantly surprised by an unplanned gain than to be disappointed in results dependent on aggressive thinking.

Renovation expenses are indicated nearly 100 percent of the time. At one end of the spectrum, even a property in excellent condition needs some staging for resale. On the other end, properties that are financially distressed are often physically distressed as well. Your objective is to know, or have someone on your investment team who will know, what it will take to make the property safe, functional, and attractive for you or for your tenant or succeeding buyer. If you have construction skills, including carpentry, plumbing, and electrical, you have an advantage over competing investors who have to hire these and other skills. Having personal knowledge in these areas or experience with renovation projects will help improve your accuracy when estimating costs, and if you can do the actual work, this will help to control your costs. There are circumstances where the buyer of a distressed property will seek to flip it in "as is" condition, but most investors tend to want to gain from the additional markup generated by making the property more attractive to a larger number of prospective buyers. One must be prudent about renovation expenses to maximize profitability. If you are in the business of flipping property after renovating it, time frames may also be important. If you have taken out a loan to acquire the property, you will reduce expenses by completing renovations expeditiously and remarketing the home as soon as possible. You will also reduce other ongoing expenses outlined in the next paragraph.

Other expenses to be considered include transfer taxes and closing, including legal costs upon purchase and resale; brokerage commission upon resale; and ongoing ownership expenses such as interest payments to a lender, insurance, real estate property taxes, utilities, and routine repairs and maintenance. It's not unusual for even the savvy investor to overlook some of these costs.

Resale price is the final piece of the puzzle. Whether a property is held for fifteen minutes or fifteen years the selling price ultimately completes the transaction. Again, market knowledge is the key. If you don't have it, make sure you have someone on your team who does. If you are in a deal for the short or intermediate term, it is possible to have a very good handle on a projected selling price at the time you are actually trying to acquire the property. Investors for the long term or those who intend to purchase the property for personal use rely on historical housing trends to expect considerably higher prices, but of course market conditions vary from time to time, and there are no guarantees. Ideally, long-term investors and homeowners dispose of property when market conditions favor the seller.

In the simplest possible terms, profit comes from the difference between selling price and purchase price plus costs. This controllable margin can be improved by investing in renovations to make the property more marketable at a higher price, by market appreciation over varying lengths of investment term, and by rental income that exceeds carrying costs over any period of ownership. Profit is reduced by poorly conceived renovation expenses, imprudent carrying costs, and carrying time that extends beyond the necessary period of ownership.

7

A WORD ABOUT RISK

Risk is a peculiar word with many connotations. Generally, it is thought to represent the possibility of taking a chance on an event that could cause a loss. Flying in an airplane, riding in a car, or even crossing a street is thought by some to have some risk, albeit a minimal one. Some people define risk as the bad side of a chance and reward as the good side; hence, the term *risk/reward* is used.

In business, **risk** may be defined as representing both good or bad. Drilling for oil is risky: you'll make money with a hit, lose money with a miss. So the risk goes in both directions.

In buying a house you take several risks:

1. Physical condition
2. Future value
3. Interest rates
4. Rental rates
5. Liquidity/marketability
6. Future events

You can try to take steps to minimize risk, including due diligence (study before buying) and insurance.

Physical condition. The physical condition of a house is important. Investigate its structural soundness, electrical and mechanical systems, and need for repairs. There are professional house inspectors who can help. An inspector can determine whether the house has contaminants such as asbestos (preferably remove it or encapsulate it), lead-based paint, urea formaldehyde insulation, or underground storage tanks (remove). Disclosure laws require sellers to tell what they know. Inspectors can test for radon in the air or water; they can find out whether the house has experienced water damage or a fire (the opportunity to inspect homes sold at foreclosure may be limited).

16

Future value. Will the house appreciate or decline in value? Because real estate is a prisoner of its location, it is important to investigate the neighborhood. Is it declining, stable, or on the upswing? Is the local and national economy weak or strong? Is the neighborhood dependent on one major employer? If so, are that employer and its industry healthy? Generally, a diversified economy is preferred. If the area is growing, what is the likelihood of its experiencing overbuilding that would depress prices?

Interest rates. These have an extensive effect on real estate. Rising rates may stop or slow new construction and may negatively affect your ability to resell. Falling interest rates could be a sign of economic weakness. Lower rates may provide an opportunity for you to refinance and reduce the payments, although there are costs involved.

Rental rates. Economic conditions may cause rental rates to rise or fall. You will need to achieve a certain rent just to break even (pay interest and operating expenses). Determine what occupancy rate and rental rate you need to break even, and get a good sense of how likely that is to be achieved. If the rent is not enough to break even, then you will need another financial benefit, such as appreciation in value, to justify the purchase.

Liquidity/marketability. Can this property be resold easily and quickly? Get a sense of how easily it can be marketed, especially if there is a possibility that you will need to sell unexpectedly or in a hurry. The amount of sales activity in the market is an indicator of liquidity.

Future events. Although we can't predict the future, try to envision what might happen down the road. Is the home on a busy or noisy street that is worsening? Or is it in a quiet, stable neighborhood? Is it in a hurricane-prone area, in a floodplain, or near a geological fault line? Have many storms or earthquakes hit the area through the years? Do the houses have wood shingle roofs that are prone to fires? Are these risks insurable? At what cost? Although you can't protect against all risks, avoid properties that bring more risk than you care to assume. And even if a risk is insurable, there is an expense to insure, plus plenty of inconvenience if the event occurs.

8

RECOGNIZING A BUYERS' MARKET

A big part of getting a bargain in any market is buying when market conditions favor buyers over sellers. This occurs when sellers are relatively competitive but buyers are not. When there are a lot of people wanting to sell houses compared with the number of willing buyers, sellers have to be much more accommodating if they wish to be successful. In fact, it is the anxious or desperate seller that bargain-conscious buyers seek out.

When buyers have the upper hand in negotiations, the market is said to be a *buyers' market.* The classic buyers' market features a lot of sellers who must sell, mainly because they must move to another city or they need the sale to complete a purchase of a bigger home. At the same time, buyers have a lot of discretion about what and when they purchase. They can afford to wait until the price is right.

Of course, the opposite situation also occurs. A *sellers' market* exists when there are a lot of buyers who need a home while sellers have the discretion to wait for the best price. In a sellers' market, it is not unusual for sellers to receive more than one offer on a home shortly after it is exposed to the market. Obviously, in such a situation, few true bargains will be found (although it might be possible in certain "turnaround" neighborhoods).

In a buyers' market, conditions may not appear very favorable for investment. The city may be losing population and struggling economically. Mortgage loans may be hard to find. The thing to keep in mind is that these conditions are likely to change over time. The seeds of many real estate empires were sown during the Depression of the 1930s when prices were low, loans were scarce, and people were trying to unload property. The people who had cash, access to capital, and the foresight to buy real estate eventually ended up with excellent investments.

Here are some things to look for that may indicate a buyers' market:

- Concentrations of "For Sale" signs, particularly when the broker's name changes every three to six months. In depressed markets caused by the closure of a major employer, whole neighborhoods may go on sale as people are forced to move for economic reasons.
- Newspaper stories about layoffs and indications of local businesses shutting down.
- Reports of high mortgage foreclosure rates. A preliminary sign of rising foreclosures is the loan delinquency rate (the percentage of loans in which payments are one to three months in arrears). Information on delinquency rates for many metropolitan areas can be purchased from the Mortgage Bankers Association at www.mbaa.com.
- Widespread evidence of price markdowns. Advertisements will report "price reduction," or similar language. Overpriced real estate can occur in any market, but in a depressed market, overpricing will be common, simply because sellers were getting those prices before the slump. Eventually, sellers give up and price the home to the market in an attempt to spark interest among buyers.
- Lots of open houses. In a slow market, agents will be trying every tactic available to drum up business.
- Lack of new construction. When markets begin to slow, new homes begun during a period of strong demand are completed and enter the inventory. There is a tendency for construction to lag the market cycle. Builders are encouraged when the market peaks, but it takes time to produce new homes. Therefore, a lot of production shows up too late. This added supply tends to further soften the market. When few buyers materialize to absorb the new supply, the flow will stop. This is a signal that the time is right for bargain hunting.
- Auctions. In this country, real estate auctions often are a sign of distressed property. When auctions become a common event, it probably means that sales through traditional means are difficult. At the same time, large inventories of repossessed real estate often are offered at an auction.

- Unfavorable terms on mortgage loans. In slow markets, the collateral value of real property is lessened. Faced with rising foreclosures, lenders are not as enthusiastic about making new loans. Consequently, they make only the ones with the lowest risk, meaning those with low loan-to-value ratios, high discount points, and tough qualifying criteria. A buyers' market favors those with top-notch credit ratings and ample cash.

It is important to understand that a market might not be a pure buyers' or sellers' market, but may be anywhere on the scale between these extremes. You may not find all the characteristics listed above, but conditions should be more in the direction described than the opposite. Any tendency toward these conditions will favor the buyer.

Likewise, if you buy in a buyers' market, do not expect to make a quick profit by turning the property over. When you go to sell, the market is working against you, unless the cycle quickly reverses. It may take anywhere from two to eight years for the market to shift. If you are buying for personal use, this probably will not be a problem, because the average holding period for owner-occupied homes is seven to ten years. If you intend to rent out the home, you may have to endure several years of high vacancy and poor rent production before demand recovers. The bargain-conscious investor must be prepared to endure such periods. In fact, this may be a time when additional investment is required to upgrade your ability to find decent tenants.

Finally, there is a chance that, instead of the market cycling, it actually is in irretrievable decline. If this is the case, the value of the property will not recover, but will only decrease. This rarely happens with whole cities (there is such a thing as a ghost town, formed when the one economic activity that created a boomtown suddenly shuts down), but it may happen to specific areas of a city. Look for things that indicate fundamental change in how the neighborhood is used. For example, if homes in the area are being converted to commercial use, it could mean value decline for the properties that remain residential. Physical conversion of single-family homes to apartments and group quarters is another sign of permanent change. In these instances, the "bargain" home may actually be fairly priced, or even overpriced.

9

BUYING OUT OF SEASON

One way to improve your chances of getting a good price on a home is to buy at the right time of year. Home prices tend to show what economists call "seasonal variation." In other words, there is a consistent pattern in home prices that appears year after year. The chart shows how median home prices, as reported by the National Association of Realtors®, have varied by month from June 2006 to May 2007. This demonstrates seasonality, though it may well include other economic factors that influenced prices during that time.

Exhibit 1
Home Prices Tend to Change According to Season*

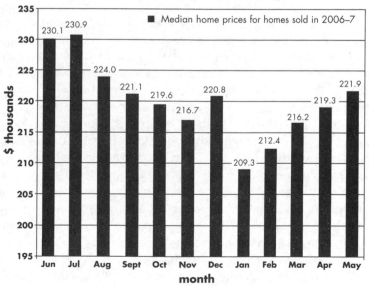

*Median home price, homes sold in 2006–7. National Association of Realtors®.

As shown, prices tend to peak in the summer and to be lowest in the winter. The main reason for this pattern is the greater number of homebuyers in the market during the late spring and early summer months. Keep in mind that the data shown are for closings, so the price reported in any one month reflects a transaction that was agreed upon from a few weeks to several months earlier. With more competition for the homes on the market, prices rise. This is sort of a mini-version of the longer-range change from a buyers' to sellers' market. Consider the spring and summer to be "mini–sellers' markets."

Likewise, the winter may be a better time to buy; a mini–buyers' market, in a sense. There are fewer buyers competing for homes. Why the variation in buyers from season to season? Some of it has to do with the reasons people move, and hence buy a home. Job transfers can occur in any season, but employees who have some say in the decision often prefer to relocate during the summer. The same goes for those who are moving to improve their housing situation. Conditions are more pleasant for house hunting and for moving during the spring. Many families with school-age children try to time a move so as not to disrupt the school year. The children do not have to be uprooted from one school to another while classes are ongoing.

Likewise, house buying and moving are to be avoided at year end. Notice in the chart that prices tend to rise a bit at the end of the year, after a big decline in the fall. Some of this rise is merely the tendency for prices to rise over time regardless of season. But some of the rise may reflect the desire of some buyers to reward themselves with a special Christmas present of a new home.

At any rate, the best time to get a bargain appears to be during the first few months of the year. One possible downside to this strategy, aside from the rigors of touring homes during the winter, is the reduction in the number of homes on the market at that time of year. After all, most people put their home on the market because they, themselves, are buying a new home. Therefore, some of the same timing dynamic works on the supply side as on the demand side. So you may not find the same variety of choices as you might later in the year. On the other hand, if your strategy is to find the most motivated sellers, you will probably have more luck in the winter. Many of these homes either sat on the market during the previous year without being sold or the sellers got into the market too late. Either way, the reality of knowing they are not in the best negotiating position will make sellers much more receptive to low, but reasonable, offers.

10

FOR SALE BY OWNER

With real estate brokerage commissions in the 4 to 7 percent range, some homeowners, in an effort to "avoid the middleman," will sell the home themselves. There is a chance that sellers unaided by a professional may price the home at a discount, effectively passing the "savings" to the buyer. In most cases, you shouldn't expect to get the entire discount. After all, the seller is taking on the work of making a sale. Negotiating somewhere in the middle can still provide a bargain price.

There is also a possibility that an owner has mispriced his or her home and is offering it for sale far below its market value. Be prepared to move quickly when you spot a bargain for sale by owner (FSBO or "fizz-bo"), because others may do the same. There are sellers, however, who have an inflated impression of the value of their property. They list high and refuse to come down. Pass these by, as they probably will be a waste of time.

Although some owners are intimidated by the thought and process of selling a house, others are not. They simply would rather not deal with a broker. They know that lawyers and title companies will assure transfer of legal title and avoid ownership minefields. Should you "lowball" these sellers, making an extremely low offer in hopes of getting a maximum bargain? Only if you are not seriously considering the property, but would buy it at a rock-bottom price. When dealing directly with a seller, it is important to go out of your way not to anger the person if you truly want to negotiate a deal. A person selling a home may have some emotional involvement in the process.

There are even real estate brokers who specialize in helping owners do everything themselves. They provide a kit with a yard sign, sample contracts to complete, and help for the seller at a flat fee or low percentage rate. Typically, they do not advertise or show the house, though those services can be contracted at additional cost. There is even the beginning of a type of Multiple

Listing Service for FSBOs using the Internet. Check www.forsalebyowner.com and www.owners.com, two sites that work much like broker-sponsored home search sites.

Dealing directly with an owner can be effective. There will not be a broker to interpret or misinterpret a spoken statement or intent. Closing, possession, and moving dates can be arranged face-to-face, without a middleman trying to recall exactly what his principal said. On the other hand, without a broker acting as a buffer, words can be misinterpreted as too harsh, causing the proposed deal to fall through. Be prepared to deal with inexperienced sellers by having your own contract forms, including the disclosures required in many states. You will have to be prepared to do all the things a buyer needs to do before closing, such as making sure that inspections are made and the financing is ready.

The matter of holding the deposit money can be a problem. Do not give the money directly to the seller. Get a trusted third party, such as a title company, to do this. The deposit is then applied in accordance with the contract, according to the title company's interpretation of the contract.

An attorney and/or title company will be used in the sale of any home. The absence of a broker should not adversely affect a knowledgeable, experienced buyer who gets help from an appraiser, home inspector, or lender. The lender will not finance the purchase of a house that is overpriced or has serious legal flaws. Therefore, the feeling of security one may get from a broker's involvement is often brought about by others in the transaction. In some circumstances, the absence of a broker can simplify the buying process as well as provide you with a bargain.

If you are committed to a broker as your representative (serving as a buyer's broker), you can still consider FSBOs. Many sellers are willing to pay the broker's commission in exchange for completing a sale.

11

WHY THE LOW PRICE? SELLER, HOUSE, OR NEIGHBORHOOD

When buying a foreclosed or bargain house, you must be especially mindful of the reason for its attractive price. Three major possibilities exist for a low price:

1. An anxious, motivated, or ignorant seller
2. Poor physical condition of the house
3. Problems in the neighborhood

The seller. Ideally, you want a house where something has gone wrong with the seller. This may sound a little callous, but keep in mind that buying out the interest of someone who is in over his head is actually a beneficial thing. The seller may be a private individual or family who is ignorant of price, needs to sell quickly, or has little at stake in the price. It may be an institution that has foreclosed or a relocation company. Someone else will absorb the loss from a quick sale. After you buy, prior owners go away, so you will hope there is nothing wrong with the house itself or its neighborhood.

The house. The house may have adverse physical characteristics that cause a problem. It could be a poorly built new house (substandard labor and materials) or a functionally obsolete older house (no insulation, too few bathrooms, inadequate wiring or plumbing, no provision for off-street parking of two cars). It may be in need of physical repairs—for example, replacement of floor coverings or window treatments, paint inside and out, facade repair, roof replacement, or structural repair. It may need costly electrical or plumbing repair.

To determine whether such a house is a bargain, start with the estimated market value if everything were in good condition; then subtract the cost of repairs. Houses are generally repairable—at some cost.

The neighborhood. Unlike sellers (whom you may never see again) or houses (generally repairable), there is nothing you can do about the neighborhood. If the neighborhood is in a downward trend, stay away. The downturn may be evidenced by a high rate of crime, serious crimes, low-scoring schools, poor area employment prospects, high unemployment rates, very low income levels, or a high proportion of residents living in substandard or public housing. At some future time, conditions may improve—but you might not be able to wait that long, and you can exercise no control over the neighborhood.

Instead, look for a stable or improving neighborhood. This will have a high percentage of owner-occupied homes, average or better schools, low crime rates, and steady or strong employment in the region.

Employment is important for two reasons:

1. People want to live in places where there is economic opportunity.
2. Jobs provide the local area with income to spend on housing and other goods.

The employment opportunities need not be within the immediate neighborhood, but they should be within an easy commute, either by car or, in the case of low- or moderate-income areas, by public transportation.

When employment prospects are bleak because a major employer or industry has closed or moved, housing prices will decline. Whether they are a bargain depends on prospects for recovery. If the economic downturn is temporary or cyclical, bargains can be had. But beware of permanent declines.

12

WHY SOME HOMES ARE UNDERVALUED

Some houses may sell for less than others in the neighborhood because they possess one or more undesirable features. As a bargain-seeking homebuyer, you will need to learn to see the potential in cosmetically unappealing homes and distinguish those from houses that are hopelessly flawed. If you are buying it for the long term and plan to rent it to a tenant, such a house may be perfectly acceptable. Renters may not be as fussy as buyers. In fact, a feature such as being on a bus line could be a positive factor for a renter, whereas a buyer might prefer to avoid the busy street. So, as a buyer-investor, you might seek out houses that are appreciated more by renters than by potential buyers.

Low prices may result from factors in these general areas:

1. Physical depreciation
   - Short-lived assets
   - Long-lived assets
2. Functional obsolescence
3. Economic/external obsolescence

See if you can identify the principal reasons why the house you recently visited hasn't sold and whether it is undervalued or priced correctly when you take the defect(s) into account. Flaws could fall into any of the following categories:

Physical depreciation*—short-lived assets: paint, carpet/floor covering, wallpaper, curtains, furnace/air-conditioning, appliances, and roof covering.

Physical depreciation—long-lived assets: studs, underground piping, foundation walls, and insulation.

*The reader should be aware that the term *depreciation* is used here to describe an economic loss in value. This is distinguished from the accounting or income tax use of *depreciation expense* as a deduction to allocate the cost of an asset over its estimated life or other period of time allowed by income tax law.

Functional obsolescence (depending on tastes in the area): absence of air-conditioning, carport or single-car garage, poor floor plan, inadequate wiring, small rooms, too many or too few bathrooms, undersized kitchen, and ceilings too low or too high.

External economic or environmental obsolescence (from outside the property): nearby noise from traffic or trains, pollution, commercial property, nuisances, eyesores, overhead wires, substandard schools, and substandard municipal services.

In most cases, reducing the depreciation of short-lived items can be achieved economically. Long-lived items are more costly. Many functional problems can be corrected.

There is a concept in depreciation called *curability*. Does the proposed cure to correct a defect make economic sense? That is, does the cost to cure add more to the value than its own cost? Curability is an economic concept. Any problem can be fixed, but is it worth the cost of repair?

Suppose a house has an outmoded kitchen. The cost to modernize the kitchen is $10,000. The house is worth $100,000 as is. If modernizing the kitchen would elevate its market value to more than $110,000, then the defect is considered curable. But don't spend $10,000 if the result is a house worth only $105,000.

There is no such thing as a perfect house. The idea is to buy one at a bargain price that is likely to appreciate through the years.

Sometimes a house languishes on the market long after it is listed. Maybe it is not what most buyers are looking for, or maybe it was overpriced and the seller initially resisted lowering the price. Selling agents lose interest in such "tired" listings and do not market them energetically. If the home fits your criteria, you may find a very motivated seller who will work with you to make the deal fit your needs.

13

RESEARCHING TARGETED PROPERTIES

Once you have identified a property that you believe represents a bargain, you are challenged to find out everything you
possibly can about your prospective purchase before you expose
a considerable investment sum. If a property is listed by a real
estate agent or broker, you may be relatively certain that the
listing price is based on reasonably careful scrutiny of its condition and marketability, then compared to recent sales of similar
homes in similar locations, called *comps*. Variables include the
expertise of the real estate agent or broker, pricing requirements
of a lender reluctantly owning the property and needing to minimize loan losses, and the unforeseen physical challenges that
may be exposed by a contractor or professional home inspector.

The good news about buying a bank-owned or other bargain
home through a real estate agent is that you will have an opportunity to inspect the premises, and you will have the opportunity
to negotiate a second inspection, bringing a contractor or home
inspector. The second inspection may include electrical, mechanical, plumbing, and structural integrity, plus environmental testing
of the drinking quality of the water and for radon in the water or
air, lead paint, insects and other pests, septic system, and
hazardous waste. Before you even get to that point, states have
varying regulations with respect to homeowner disclosures. By the
time you enter into an agreement of sale, the agent is likely to
have presented you with disclosure information supplied by the
homeowner. If the homeowner is a person or people, they are
duty-bound to provide accurate information, though often data is
unreliable or stated as "unknown." If a property is bank- or
lender-owned, the representative of the lender has never lived in
the home, so you may count on a disclosure riddled with
"unknowns." The buyer must always beware, but at least in a

home that is listed with a broker, you will be able to access the premises at least once.

Evaluating homes that are scheduled for foreclosure presents the real challenge. Unless the home is already on the market or becomes listed with a broker as a pre-foreclosure, at the point where the legal notice is issued, there should be little or no expectation of ever gaining access to the premises before bidding on the property. There may be creative ways of approaching the homeowner to gain access, but it is very rare for the lender who is foreclosing to afford prospective bidders a look inside. Homes that are being foreclosed are more likely to reveal problems upon inspection than they are to please the prospective buyer with unanticipated amenities. Where they may have discretion in nonjudicial foreclosures, lenders learned long ago that they are more likely to turn off bidders than they are to generate higher interest by permitting entry. In many cases where the homeowner and lender are at odds, the lenders just don't have the keys or permission to enter. In judicial foreclosures, no court is going to force the borrower to exhibit their property.

So how does a prospective bidder acquire information about the quality and marketability of a property noticed for foreclosure before attending the foreclosure sale? There are a number of means for gathering factual information and for generating an impression that will help you decide whether to pursue a given property. Acting on any of these sources will help. Pursuing all of them will give you the best chance to know the property on which you will be bidding.

1. The drive-by
2. The tax assessor's office
3. The tax collector
4. A real estate professional
5. The homeowner
6. The neighbors
7. The registry of deeds

The drive-by is as simple as getting in your car and driving to the property noticed for sale. You are going to have to determine whether the house is in a neighborhood with a good future, or if the property is better situated for short-term resale. The condition of the exterior and yard will lend insight into what you might

31

expect the interior condition to be. If a property is absolutely meticulous, ready for resale tomorrow, then there is a chance that the interior is also well maintained. There are no guarantees. If a property is obviously not well maintained outside, prepare your psyche for lots of work and the possibility of unwelcome surprises on the inside. It is always safest to allot generous rehab time and a financial contingency fund for the unforeseen. You are bidding on a property in "as is" condition. The borrower has no duty to turn over the home in good condition. They can be angry and destructive. In some cases when a home already has been vacated, there may have been vandalism, frozen pipes, or damage from other causes. You never know until you gain access.

The **tax assessor's office** can be found at city or town hall, or in some cases at county offices. Information on the property may also be available online, at the tax assessor's Web site. Property information typically contains a tax assessment card (computerized, print, or both) offering a wealth of information that may include, but is not limited to, the following:

- The age of the house
- The number of rooms
- The number of full, half, or three-quarter bathrooms
- The number of fireplaces
- Flooring (carpet vs. wood or tile)
- Effective square footage
- Type of heat system and fuel used
- Capacity of electrical system
- Public or private water system
- Public sewage or private septic
- Exterior building materials
- Roofing materials
- Lot size
- Frontage

These are important physical characteristics that will add significantly to the impression gathered during your drive-by. Another critical element on many tax cards is an area that addresses "condition" of the property. Assessors may adjust home values determined strictly from building qualities and spatial measurements on the basis of their perception of the condition in which the house is maintained. Assessors may not always see the inside of a home, or their viewings may be dated, so there is always a question about how much to rely on the assessor's statement of condition. Upgrades may have been made without the assessor's knowledge, but if you see indication that condition at any time was fair or poor, or that a ratio applied to the assessment formula was well below 100 percent, this is a concern. You may want to check to see if building permits have ever been pulled to address renovation needs. In smaller markets, the tax assessor may have personal familiarity with the home you have identified for possible purchase. In such cases, the assessor is a good person to know and a potentially good research source.

There is also great financial information that can be found on tax cards or elsewhere in the tax assessor's office, including the Web site. The most recent and/or historical selling prices of the subject property may appear on the tax card. You should also be able to find records of recent sales in the same city or town that you can use to develop comparative prices and estimate resale values. You can organize comps by location and house type (colonial, ranch, contemporary, and so on); by numbers of rooms or bedrooms; by square footage; by condition; and by the amount of accompanying land. The amount of the tax assessment depicted on each tax card can give you a general sense of value, but properties are rarely sold at their assessed value. It is actually more important to know the typical difference between recent selling prices and the assessed value in order to effectively estimate resale value. For example, you may learn that assessments are 10 to 15 percent below selling prices. The more properties in your calculation sample, particularly those that are true comps, the more accurate your estimate should be. In the absence of help from a real estate professional, the data available in the assessor's office are extremely important.

The **tax collector** can tell you not only the amount of annual property taxes to be paid on the property in which you have an interest, but also whether any taxes are outstanding. Even if liens do not appear during title work, property taxes survive the foreclosure process and become the liability of the buyer. You will not be able to resell the property until property taxes are redeemed. Also, be sure to ask if there are any unpaid water or sewer bills if these services are public. If public water and sewer services are not managed at the city or town hall, they will refer you to the provider. Like property taxes, these levies will survive a foreclosure.

A real estate professional, either a broker or an agent, is great to have on your acquisition team. If the property is already listed, you may be able to obtain much of the information discussed above on a listing sheet and from accompanying materials and disclosures. You should also be able to visit a listed premises. Under a listing agreement, your agent may be able to co-broker the sale and receive compensation from the seller. If the property is not currently listed, your agent might be able to provide you with historical listing data from the local multiple listing service. Previous listing forms will shed light on physical qualities and condition, previous asking and selling prices, and the number of days the property had been on the market before selling, a clue to customer interest in the future. Going a step further, contacting a previous listing agent means you or your agent may be able to learn of physical or other drawbacks to the property.

The homeowner can be viewed as either the enemy or an interesting ally. Key 19 discusses how to approach the homeowner or borrower during the pre-foreclosure period. If your courage permits, organizing a meeting with the homeowner before foreclosure may afford you and your agent or contractor an opportunity to inspect the premises before bidding at foreclosure auction. When the meeting has the potential for hostility, it is always advisable to take someone with you. In this case an agent or contractor will not only serve as a witness and counselor, but also generate a second opinion from a valued professional.

The neighbors can be an added source of information. In many cases they have been inside the house and can lend insight. Chances are they know if there has been a fire or when the basement last flooded. Neighbors can also provide information about the neighborhood that can aid in your efforts to resell the property.

The registry of deeds is where you can research obligations of the borrower who is being foreclosed. Foreclosing lenders or their representatives will advertise and make available the mortgage that is the subject of the foreclosure. By viewing it, you can learn the original amount of the borrower's loan and whether the lender has further exposure by paying taxes and insurance on behalf of the borrower. You are unlikely to learn the actual amount of the lender's total exposure (outstanding principal, taxes, insurance, foreclosure marketing expenses) before auction day, and you will learn it only if the lender (or agent) decides to bid. If you are able to make an educated guess about what the lender's bid may be, it may determine whether or not you actually attend the auction. If the estimated lender exposure is too close to your estimated resale price, it may not be worth your time.

The registry of deeds is the more important place to conduct borrower research because, in addition to viewing the mortgage to be foreclosed, you can view all other recorded borrower obligations in connection with the subject property. You can determine whether you are bidding on a first mortgage, sometimes called a *mortgage of precedence*, which is always preferable. If you successfully bid on a second or later mortgage, you are still going to have to work through any lien of precedence before you can assume control of the foreclosed property. At the registry you may also learn of municipal liens for unpaid property taxes, water and sewer bills, or other obligations, though it is always best to check with the local tax collector before bidding. Such obligations transfer to the successful foreclosure bidder before the property can be resold. It is not unusual for struggling borrowers to become indebted to the Internal Revenue Service. There are special provisions the IRS may or may not choose to exercise to step into the shoes of a foreclosure buyer if an IRS lien of significant value has been recorded. If the target property is a condominium, or in an association where cooperative fees are gathered, depending on state law and how the documents are constructed, there may or may not be an obligation to assume recorded liens. Generally, all liens recorded at the registry of deeds that predate the mortgage being foreclosed continue to be obligations of the succeeding property owner. When there are liens recorded after the mortgage, mechanic's and other liens may be extinguished by foreclosure, but IRS and municipal liens are not extinguished. It is advisable to conduct title research or pay to have it conducted at the registry before bidding. If you learn of other mortgages and recorded liens, guidance from a real estate attorney is advised.

14

INSPECTING
THE PROPERTY

When possible, you should inspect a property thoroughly before making an offer. Repossessed or bank-owned property is usually available for inspection. Foreclosure auctions, however, will not offer the opportunity to inspect the interior. When you are buying repossessed property, such an inspection is even more important, since it may be difficult or impossible to insert an addendum into the sales contract to cover repairs. In addition, many repossessed homes have sat vacant for extended periods (some may even have been vandalized by their previous owners) and may need repairs and remedial upkeep. You will want to know about such conditions before you bid because the condition of the property will affect how much you bid or even if you bid at all.

Since you are concerned about what a property is worth—even if the home is ideally suited to you, there is no need to bid more than market value—you should inspect the property from the viewpoint of an appraiser. This means you want to look at several different factors that affect the property's market value. The most logical way to approach this is to start with the more general and move to the specific. This also provides the advantage of allowing you to screen out properties without going through an entire analysis. In fact, at the more general levels, you can consider more than one property at a time.

Let's say that you want to invest locally and have settled on the general area. You should develop some idea of what neighborhoods are the most desirable for the type of property you want to own. You should check out the location from the standpoint of how convenient it is to employment centers and other areas of interest. This should be evaluated from the viewpoint of your lifestyle (if you plan to occupy the home) or that of your prospective tenants (if you plan to rent out the home). For example, access to public transportation may be important for college students or the elderly.

Next, look at the residential quality of the neighborhood. Is it attractive? Is there too much traffic? Are there conveniently located parks? Do people maintain their homes well? Does the area appear to be changing in its use (encroaching commercial uses, vacant buildings, conversions of single-family homes to apartments)? The home you are considering may be in excellent condition. However, a deteriorating neighborhood will frustrate the best maintenance program. As an individual homeowner, there is little you can do about it.

Look at how the property fits into the neighborhood. Is there a great amount of conformity? Do surrounding homes have features that the subject lacks, or vice versa? In general, it is better to be deficient (and pay less) if the home can be brought up to the area standards without great expense. Adding features that are uncommon to the neighborhood will do little to improve the value of the home.

Finally, examine the home. You may want to employ a professional home inspector to help you at this stage. The inspector will check out the plumbing, mechanical, and electrical components of the home and point out any deficiencies and defects. You may need a second inspector, a structural engineer, for the foundation. A good inspector should be able to find things that might take you several years to discover. Make a list of things that can be repaired economically and things that would cost too much to do (such as changing an awkward floor layout). You can estimate the cost of doing the repairs and the reduced value of putting up with those features that cannot be changed.

If you can contact the previous owner, do so to ask about the condition of the property. You may also ask neighbors whether they know of any defects. Perhaps they have had discussions about foundation repairs, termite treatment, a fire or flood. If the house is in a small town where there are few repair services, you could call these services to inquire.

In addition to the physical inspection, it is worthwhile to check the public record for any outstanding taxes. Any back taxes due the city, county, school district, or other governmental unit carry over to the new owner. The same is true of homeowner association dues and assessments that have not been paid. Failure to make these debts good can result in loss of property when the government liens are enforced.

This information will be helpful when you are preparing a bid (see Key 33). It may be that you can avoid bidding at all, if the property is not suitable or has too many problems. In fact, you may write off entire neighborhoods based on your initial evaluations.

15

WINNING WITH REPOSSESSED HOMES

Possibly the ultimate motivated seller is the one who acquired the home as a consequence of a failed business agreement. Such is the case of lending institutions, mortgage insurance companies, and others who stand behind the borrower's obligation to repay the loan. When the borrower defaults, one of these institutions likely will end up with the property.

These entities acquire properties to try to recover their investment in the loan. Their hope is to resell the property as soon as possible for enough money to repay the loan principal, accrued interest, and expenses of recovery. Time is of the essence, in most cases. They tend to be very cooperative with the interested buyer. Typically, they have processes in place for accepting bids and occasionally place properties at auction. Most of these properties are listed with brokers, and it is not always possible to identify them as foreclosures. Often, however, you can locate these properties from the selling institution's Web site.

Among these institutions are those that hold mortgages. Some are depository institutions, such as banks and savings and loan associations, that originate loans and hold them in portfolio. When a borrower defaults, the lender may foreclose the loan and either take over the property in a nonjudicial foreclosure or purchase the property at a foreclosure sale held as part of a judicial foreclosure. Similarly, mortgage investors may acquire properties when the mortgages they hold are foreclosed. Nowadays, however, most lending institutions don't own the loans that they have originated. They have sold the loans to national mortgage investors, though they may continue to service the loans, often because the property is in their locale. The biggest national mortgage investors are the federally sponsored organizations Fannie Mae and Freddie Mac. National mortgage investors or mortgage insurers will have policies and procedures that the loan servicer must observe. This typically means that the repossessed property may be marketed by local real estate brokers.

Many mortgage loans require mortgage insurance that protects the lender in the case of borrower default. When such insurance is in effect, the insuring or guaranteeing organization generally acquires the property after foreclosure. These organizations include private mortgage insurers such as the Mortgage Guaranty Insurance Corporation (MGIC) as well as the public Federal Housing Administration (FHA) and Department of Veterans Affairs (VA). Also, the Federal Deposit Insurance Corporation (FDIC), which insures deposit accounts in banks and savings and loans, acquires properties in the course of liquidating failed lending institutions.

Anyone interested in bargain properties should become familiar with the procedures required to buy from these organizations. Often, the properties are marketed under listing contracts, just like most other properties on the market. Therefore, one avenue to explore is inquiries with local real estate agents. Holders of large inventories of properties will have methods by which a prospective buyer can place bids on properties. Often, sealed bids are accepted over a specific period of time and the best qualifying bid is accepted. Other Keys in this book provide more detail on how each of the major holders of repossessed homes operates.

There are several advantages of buying homes through these procedures:

- In many cases, the properties have been upgraded to comply with local codes or to the standard required to get financing or insurance from the selling institution. Buyers, however, should always inspect the properties before committing. (One caveat in dealing with repossessed property is that the institutions and firms that sell these homes are not subject to the property condition disclosure requirements that apply to individual sellers.)
- Some sellers offer financing, often at favorable terms. In this way, the holder of the property hopes to turn a bad debt into a new performing loan. Unless you plan to pay cash, the opportunity to get financing can be valuable.

- Organizations with government ties, such as the FHA, Fannie Mae, and Freddie Mac, may have special deals for certain types of buyers or for homes in certain locations. For example, some give priority to buyers who plan to occupy the home, to first-time homebuyers, or to those bidding on homes in depressed neighborhoods.
- Some sellers may be willing to pay a portion of the closing costs normally paid by the buyer.

Although institutions are highly interested in getting rid of these properties, they are not panic sellers: they are not willing to give them away. Usually, they will try to get all or a large proportion of what they have invested in the property. If the bids are not high enough, they may wait for better ones to come in. It is important to do the homework required to fairly price the properties. If you want to bid low, in hopes of getting the best price, you should be prepared to lose out most of the time. Usually, if the organization wants a quick sale, it will call an auction for a group of properties. Even then, it may place a reservation price to try to limit its loss. The bidder should know the market price and the procedures of the organization offering the property.

Often, after a real estate professional has become involved, the opportunity for buying at a deep discount diminishes. The real estate agent's commission adds to the seller's costs to be recovered via a higher price, and the agent may be more knowledgeable about market prices.

The bottom line with REO (Real Estate Owned) properties is that you probably will not get a home at a rock-bottom price, but the procedure eliminates much of the risk of a foreclosure purchase. Foreclosed inventory may not be of much interest to the savvy investor but should be explored by those looking for a home at a reasonable price.

16

SNATCHING A HOME FROM THE JAWS OF FORECLOSURE

Foreclosure is almost always a financial catastrophe for the homeowner and often presents the lender with a loss as well. Therefore, it is in everyone's interest to avoid the event. There may be an opportunity to buy from the owner just before foreclosure. The homeowner will try to sell the home when facing difficulties in keeping up payments. However, if the sale will not yield enough money to pay off the loan, most financially strapped homeowners have little choice other than to allow foreclosure to proceed.

Knowing that foreclosure sales rarely cover the outstanding loan and expenses, lenders will sometimes try to work out a solution with a homeowner who wishes to keep the home and retains some ability to support a loan. Such a workout may involve restructuring the loan to provide lower monthly payments or even accepting a reduced payback.

When interest rates have dropped, and a lender is willing to be flexible to revive a loan, there may be an opportunity for a third party, you, to forge an attractive deal. This is particularly the case when the present homeowner clearly has no ability or intention to retain the home. You may step into the homeowner's place and break the roadblock to working out a solution that avoids foreclosure.

Such situations will be infrequent, even when foreclosures are running at above-normal levels. Many loans are held in institutional pools that may preclude any type of workout that lowers the loan value. In any case, you would need to step in before foreclosure had begun. The key to identifying such cases is a knowledgeable broker who works with homeowners and is aware of the possibilities of a pre-foreclosure sale. If you are interested in such opportunities, inform a broker you have confidence in that you might be willing to be party to a workout under the right terms. It will not be surprising if the broker has several current cases of homeowners faced with the likelihood of foreclosure. However, the broker must also be willing to contact the lender and sound out the possibilities of a workout. Another source is classified ads in the newspaper where individuals may advertise for sale by owner (FSBO). Individual owners may also plant a "For Sale" sign in their yard. It is worth a call to get more information and a feel for the market.

Before entering into negotiations, there are some bits of information you should gather. Of course you should inspect the property to see whether it is suitable for your lifestyle, just as with any other purchase. Determine your maximum price based on comparable properties and, if you intend to rent out the home, what price will be low enough to allow rent to provide a reasonable return. Make sure the loan that is being restructured is the only lien against the property. You do not want to be surprised by a bill for delinquent taxes or homeowner association dues or find out later that a second mortgage exists. Find out the terms on the existing loan and whether the lender can and will allow it to be assumed. If not, you may have to arrange outside financing. In most cases, the lender will prefer restructuring the financing if the price is right, since this may avoid the necessity of devaluing the loan on the lender's books.

A mutually beneficial match on a pre-foreclosure sale may be hard to find. However, when it does occur, it can be extremely beneficial. Think of yourself as providing the key to a win-win solution for both the lender and homeowner. But do it only if the deal also works to your benefit.

17

BANKS DON'T WANT TO OWN REAL ESTATE

Banks and other lending institutions are not prepared to own real estate. Their daily business is shuffling money and papers—not managing property. Their staff has a daily routine that consists of taking deposits and making loans. When it comes to the ownership, management, and resale of foreclosed properties, they are lacking in staff, expertise, and resources. That is why foreclosure is considered a last resort, and why banks are eager to rid themselves of foreclosed houses.

Banks must continually meet tests conceived by government regulators and applied by auditors or examiners to show that they have adequate capital to operate safely. Owning real estate other than their own buildings, called *real estate owned* (REO) or *loans through foreclosure* (LTF), is counterproductive to meeting capital tests, to the growth of their bank, and to smooth operations. Generally, bank personnel are rewarded for making good loans and servicing the loans. Owning repossessed real estate is a drag on their operations and growth. Loan officers will not be rewarded for having an inventory of foreclosed property. If bank personnel work with foreclosures, any reward will be for the quick disposal of foreclosed property, which could mean quick sales at low prices.

If you are interested in acquiring a portfolio of foreclosed houses at bargain prices, then meet and make friends with the bankers in charge of these assets at various banks in your city or town. Ask the banker to call you when a property has been or is about to be foreclosed.

Try to keep a checking or savings account at each bank. Often you will need friends or relationships at several banks because each may have a policy preventing them from financing properties that they have foreclosed but allowing them to finance others' property coming out of foreclosure. That is, you need one bank to buy from and a different one to borrow from.

This strategy may not always be possible. Most home loans are held by Fannie Mae and Freddie Mac instead of being kept in the portfolio of the originating lending institution. If this is the case, the lender may not have much to offer in the way of REO properties. It is always good to maintain friendly bank contacts. You should be able to find out quickly whether this is a fruitful avenue to pursue for a property by talking to a few local bankers.

18

IDENTIFYING PRE-FORECLOSURE PROPERTIES

Technically speaking, a property enters pre-foreclosure when legal notice is issued to the borrower. The public is generally unaware at this particular point. Sometime later, the party handling the foreclosure process, whether the court, the sheriff, the trustee, or an attorney, is caused to legally advertise the sale by foreclosure and provide notice to any known interested parties, including the registry of deeds, city or town, and any other lien holders on the subject property. Other lien holders may include, but are not limited to, other lenders, municipal services, utilities, and condominium or homeowner associations. Referring to Key 25, "Foreclosure Process by State," you can learn whether a given state conducts the majority of its foreclosures by judicial or nonjudicial means or by both, who oversees the sale, and by what date before auction sale the overseer must begin public notice. The pre-foreclosure period begins at issuance of lender's default notice to borrower and concludes when deed to the property is transferred after an auction sale.

Early awareness of a property to be foreclosed can sometimes be found at an auctioneer's Web site or printed calendar of upcoming foreclosure auction sales. There are times when an auctioneer who specializes in this field may post the information before legal notices are required to be published. More typically, prospective foreclosure buyers become aware of a property to be foreclosed when legal notices are published. There are a number of ways to keep informed of noticed properties:

- Newspapers
- Registrar of deeds
- Third-party Internet sources

- City or town tax collector
- Auctioneer advertising

Publishing of legal notices is dictated by state law or by the court overseeing the foreclosure. They specify the number of public advertising notices required and the dates by which they must appear before foreclosure sale. Generally, the court, sheriff, trustee, or attorney will choose to advertise notice in a newspaper judged to have appeal to the most interested prospective buyers and/or those who might have legal claim or interest in such notice. In some locations, the ad is purely local. In other states, there may be newspapers that, over time, the public has come to know as the main source of legal notice advertising—a dominant newspaper based in the state capital or major business center, for example. It is important to research which methodology typifies the area in which you expect to pursue foreclosures. There are no guarantees that the typical methodology will reveal all noticed properties, however.

Legal notices must also be copied to the relevant county registry of deeds. Here you should be able to assure access to complete information. If you live close to the county registry, it could be as simple as walking in and asking for the most current list of properties to be foreclosed. You may also consider purchasing a subscription to an authorized area or statewide registry publication that weekly or periodically publishes various summaries of legal information, including foreclosures. Such properties may be identified by address, name of borrower, lien holder, and the county book and page number where the mortgage instrument of foreclosure can be found. Auction sale dates and times are also identified. Authorized registry publications are available in print form, and they are increasingly available online or as electronic newsletters. They can be expensive, but they are the single tool most likely to report all noticed foreclosures in your target area.

If you are reading this book, chances are you have already been exposed to television or Internet advertising promoting foreclosure resources. There is a lot of "how-to" information, and there are also sites that offer lists of foreclosed properties, usually lender-owned property listed for resale. Realtytrac.com, Foreclosure.com, ForeclosureS.com, Preforeclosure.com,

ForeclosureList.com, and ForeclosureU.com are reasonably well-known sites at this writing. Some may also offer access to pre-foreclosure information. This specialty enjoys considerable and frequent change. You might employ a search engine at any given time to identify these and other resources. Please remember that, although these folks are selling services, their information is not always as comprehensive or as current as you should expect to find at the registry of deeds or through its authorized publication. At the same time, if you are willing to pay for some services, there is valuable research information that can be bought.

Because legal foreclosure notices are sent to the city or town where each foreclosure is located, city or town hall can also be a place where you can identify opportunities. Usually the tax collector or the tax collector's office will be aware of upcoming foreclosure auctions. Foreclosures are a matter of public interest, and property addresses, names of homeowner (borrower), and dates and times of foreclosure should be available to you for the asking. If you are not going to subscribe to a newspaper that frequently carries foreclosure notices or a registry review, the tax collector's office is a reasonably comprehensive option when a specific town or two is targeted. Be warned, however, that this method is subject to human error, or sometimes to lack of interest in cooperation with your periodic requests.

If a foreclosure is not identified by one or more of the methods above, the last opportunity to spot a property to be foreclosed usually occurs when an auctioneer advertises online, in a local newspaper, or by direct mail. This may occur in whatever news-paper the auctioneer thinks will best reach parties interested in the subject property. Because auctioneers are not always local to the property being sold, there is no guarantee that the ad will appear in the most appropriate vehicle. If you can identify all the auctioneers selling foreclosures in your targeted area, it is worth the small effort to assure that they have you on their mailing list, and it is advised that you visit their Web sites to supplement other research and to keep up to date on the status of pre-foreclosures.

19

BUYING PRE-FORECLOSURES BEFORE AUCTION

One of the worst things that can happen to a homeowner is to lose his or her home to foreclosure. If a noticed borrower is unable to restore his or her credit relationship with the lender before foreclosure sale, the next best thing to do is to sell the property, or at least place the property under a purchase agreement, before the auction date. Auctions are commonly postponed or sometimes even canceled when a property is under such agreement. If the owner can sell at an amount exceeding his or her obligations, lender(s) can be paid, and other debts may be retired. The seller may even realize a profit. More important, although the homeowner's credit history may have been damaged, it is rescued from the far uglier blemish of foreclosure. A foreclosure in a borrower's history is so important to avoid that even a breakeven or small-loss scenario should be preferable. The smartest of homeowners living under the threat of foreclosure will work fast to preserve their equity and credit rating by selling the property quickly to avoid foreclosure.

Some threatened homeowners are the victims of bad timing with respect to having borrowed an amount that may exceed declining market values, or they may have borrowed such a high percentage of the market value that economic change is not allowing them to keep payments current. Such scenarios do not usually produce good opportunities for buying or selling before auction sale. On the other hand, if you have determined that the borrower is unencumbered by secondary obligations, and the foreclosing lender's exposure is sufficiently below market value, then you may have identified a win-win opportunity for the distressed homeowner and yourself.

Legal notices, registry review summaries, and most auctioneer advertisements will reveal the county book and page number of the mortgage being foreclosed. If you do not already have the name(s) of the borrower(s), looking at the mortgage will reveal the identity of the property owner(s). You can then purchase or conduct your own registry research on the title of the subject property to review the deed and to ascertain liens and other interests. Although you cannot definitively determine the amount currently owed to the foreclosing lender, you can obtain the original loan amount on the mortgage. If you estimate that the remaining mortgage principal, plus required lender expenses such as taxes and insurance (this sum is called *lender exposure*), is well below the property's market value, and there are no liens or encumbrances that dissuade your interest, then you have identified the right conditions for a pre-foreclosure purchase. Bear in mind that all liens placed behind the non-foreclosed mortgage will survive. They may be extinguished only after an actual foreclosure auction sale. A second mortgage, for example, or some mechanic's or homeowner association liens may be ignored only after foreclosure completion. In cases where there are secondary obligations that you are unwilling to assume, it is better to allow the foreclosure sale to take place which will extinguish them, and then participate as a sale-day foreclosure bidder. Note, however, that IRS, property tax, municipal, and some homeowner association liens will survive the foreclosure.

Between research conducted at the registry of deeds and the tax assessor's information available at city hall, town hall, or county offices, you may be able to determine the borrower's original purchase price. This can be, but is not always, a useful number to have when discussing resale price. It is important to get advice from a real estate professional or to use information at the tax assessor's office to estimate current market value from comparable homes. The longer the borrower has owned a home that has appreciated, the more likely there is to be that desirable gap between current market value and lender exposure. This is a simple matter of appreciation plus the building of equity through mortgage amortization during the term of ownership. The larger the gap, the greater the likelihood that common ground can be reached for a pre-foreclosure agreement of sale.

The important question after you have identified a property ripe for a win-win pre-foreclosure negotiation is how to go about approaching the homeowner. Bearing in mind that borrowers threatened with foreclosure are usually under immense pressure and could easily be sensitive, you have to ask yourself whether you are prepared to confront a possibly angry homeowner directly. One alternative is to find a real estate professional who is willing to "door knock" the homeowner. This simply refers to an agent willing to take the initiative to contact a homeowner when the home is not on the market. There are always real estate folks who have built excellent relationships with lenders and have positioned themselves to sell lender-owned property after foreclosures. In some areas of the country where foreclosures are common, you may even find a real estate agent who specializes in the soliciting and selling of foreclosures before the deadline of an auction sale. These clever agents know how to help homeowners understand the merits of selling the home that they really don't want to lose because it suits their longer-term credit and possibly their equity interests. You may find that such an agent already has your targeted foreclosure listed for sale. In such a case, a listing agent is duty-bound to recommend a selling price closer to market value and often adjusted for obvious seller motivation. If you have done your pricing homework, you should have the underlying knowledge to at least try to negotiate a favorable, win-win offer. Agents who have less experience in pre-foreclosure work may still be beneficial to use as a buffer between you, possibly perceived as an aggressive buyer, and a likely agitated homeowner. Then you will need to screen agents, not just for their professional competence, but for their courage and hustle as well. Remember also that a benefit to working with a real estate professional is that they have all of the contract forms and the procedural knowledge to bring about a successful closing on the property.

What if you decide that you have the courage and the ability to approach the homeowner directly? Lots of buyers do. Armed with the name(s) of the homeowner(s), the address, and the knowledge that foreclosure notice has been served, you have three obvious options to make initial contact:

1. Literally knock on the door of the home.
2. Mail a letter.
3. Telephone the homeowner.

Appearing without warning at the front door of a homeowner to discuss a foreclosure notice certifies your courage but challenges good taste. It's risky! It could yield and probably has yielded results, but even if you think you know the homeowner, it is difficult to judge how foreclosure notice has affected the individual(s) and the family. This approach is not recommended, but if you must take it, it is advisable to take someone with you.

If you elect to mail an inquiry, put yourself in the shoes of the receiving reader. Try to imagine what words are going to stimulate interest versus arousing further emotion or anger. Short and sweet is good, but you are going to have to find a way to convey sympathy and understanding, express empathy, and present a strategy for a solution in concise fashion. Remember that the likely first instinct is for the homeowners to want to keep the home. Sale of the home may not have been a considered option. You want to either introduce this possibility as a solution and/or support the notion of sale as a remedy. Knowing and revealing too much can be detrimental to your game plan. Your objective should be to establish a rapport such that a telephone call, an e-mail, or even a personal meeting at the property becomes possible. There are no guarantees of a reply to the letter you send.

The more certain way of assuring bidirectional communication is via the telephone call. It's less risky than suddenly appearing at the homeowners' door. Unlike the letter to which you receive no response, telephoning at least means you are going to have the opportunity to speak with someone. It may or may not afford you the opportunity to deliver your message. If you do get to make your case, you should be able to evaluate whether or not there is an opportunity to continue any quality of dialogue.

Once you establish an agreeable level of communication, your objective should be to meet at the subject property, ultimately resulting in a tour of the home. Gaining access will help you determine your continuing level of interest, and it will guide you on budgeting for an offer. Again, it is advisable to take someone with you. It will add to the safety and emotional security of all parties. Ideally, a real estate agent or a contractor can act as your second. The insight of either professional can play a significant role in guiding your further actions. If possible, choose the professional whose skill set provides the greatest complement to your own knowledge.

Assuming you are successful at arranging a meeting, and that you have continuing interest after inspecting the premises, you must be prepared to discuss a possible sale while remaining sensitive to the likely emotions of the homeowners. Once you have been able to reason that selling is the most beneficial solution for the homeowners, you have to focus on setting a price that meets your profit objectives while simultaneously meeting the homeowners' financial needs. Remember that you may already be perceived as taking advantage of a tragic situation. You will likely have more motivation and knowledge, and the homeowners can easily feel threatened. If you start with a price offer that barely covers the mortgage and even other debts, you may get lucky, but you might also upset the prospective sellers. You really have to qualify the homeowners' financial and emotional needs to avoid alienating them in this process. Once the homeowners agree that selling is in their best interest, they are more likely to want market value than to settle for breaking even on debt obligations. The homeowners may or may not have a realistic idea of current value, and there is usually an emotional attachment that has to be overcome. Your opportunity will depend on achieving that feeling of win-win. If a price that meets your game plan also dignifies the homeowners with some walking-away money, you have a much better chance of reaching agreement.

Once agreement on a selling price is reached, terms such as closing date and inspections must also be agreed upon. Earlier closing dates benefit the sellers. If they can close before the foreclosure auction sale date, it is usually of great interest to do so. Again, borrowers under contract to sell can usually postpone an auction sale until after the contracted closing date. At closing the lender's exposure is satisfied. The foreclosure gets canceled. You will need to know how to prepare a legally acceptable agreement of sale (also known as a *contract of sale, purchase and sale agreement, or earnest money contract*). It is recommended that you retain an attorney or a real estate professional to assist you at this point. They can assure that all proper steps are taken.

Prepare yourself for rejection. Trying to buy a property before the foreclosure auction sale deadline is not easy. It takes a lot more courage than simply appearing at the auction sale with a bid card in hand. There are two benefits to taking this risky, aggressive approach. First, if you build a rapport with the homeowners before the auction, you may have a chance to erase the auction-day competition and negotiate exclusively. Your chances of getting the property at a lower price improve while you help the homeowners save future creditworthiness. Second, even if you are unable to come to agreeable terms, you may have been able to inspect the property, which you are unlikely to be able to do on auction day, and you may have been able to build a rapport that allows you to work better with the homeowners after the auction if you then become the successful bidder. In some states the successful bidder assumes the painful responsibility of removing the homeowners before taking possession. Leaving negotiations on the friendliest and most respectful of notes can be extremely important.

20

WHY HOMES ARE REPOSSESSED

Lenders are willing to make home mortgage loans for fairly large amounts and at fairly low rates of interest because a valuable piece of property makes good collateral. When you get a loan to buy a home, you sign two important documents. The first—the note—describes your obligation to repay the loan each month. The second—the mortgage contract—gives the lender certain legal rights to the home in case you fail to fulfill your obligation to repay the loan. Without the home as collateral securing the loan, no lender would consider giving you such a large loan.

Of course, not everyone who signs a mortgage contract is able to live up to the financial obligation. Loss of a job, a major financial loss, or an unexpected burden could render a borrower insolvent and unable to continue making payments. Most mortgage contracts allow a grace period of only ten to fifteen days after a payment is due before a penalty is added to the payment, and the loan is soon considered delinquent. When payments are generally three or more months behind, the loan is considered in default and the borrower is notified of the consequences of not keeping up with the payments. Local lenders sometimes work with borrowers who are having difficulty because of job loss or some other hardship, especially when it is obviously temporary. However, many loans are merely serviced by local lenders or specialized loan servicing companies, having been bought by a national institutional investor. These investors apply general policies to all loans and do not allow the local servicer to deviate from policy. After default, a lender's next step is to accelerate the loan (declare the full amount to be due immediately, not just the missed payments) and start foreclosure proceedings.

A loan can be in default and subject to foreclosure for any breach of the mortgage contract. For example, failing to insure a property adequately is a default of the mortgage contract. However, almost all foreclosures are the result of not making loan payments on time.

Although financial difficulty usually is at the root of delinquent payments, a homeowner who is unable to make payments could often sell the house and pay off the loan. If market conditions are not right, however, the borrower may not be able to sell the home for enough to cover the mortgage balance and the expenses of a sale. That is why home foreclosures are so frequent when local economies go into recession. Not only are people thrown out of work and incomes decreased, but the market values of homes fall. Under these conditions, homeowners have been known to simply mail their house keys to the lender in lieu of the monthly payment. Still, they may be liable for the difference between their debt and the eventual sales price at foreclosure, called a "deficiency judgment."

When a lender accelerates the loan, the borrower has a certain amount of time to respond to this mandate. Foreclosure is the process by which the lender turns to the collateral property to satisfy the outstanding debt. The procedures used and the rights available to the borrower are established by state law and may differ markedly from state to state. The next several Keys describe various steps in the process in general terms. For your particular state, you will need to consult an attorney familiar with local law.

Authors' note: Keys 21–30 provide information about foreclosures that may be helpful in understanding the process, but is not essential to the potential homebuyer. The homebuyer needs assurance from a qualified attorney or title company about the quality of title being received, and any risks assumed. The homebuyer must not assume those risks nor rely on information provided here as sufficient to avoid legal difficulties with acquisitions.

21

JUDICIAL FORECLOSURE

The rights of mortgage lenders and borrowers have evolved over time. The basic premise is to allow the lender to protect its investment in the event that the borrower fails to live up to the mortgage agreement. At the same time, the law aims to protect the borrower from a lender who wants to wrest away the mortgaged property wrongfully. We all have in mind a picture of the unscrupulous lender pouncing on a helpless borrower by claiming valuable property at the first sign of economic trouble. Most lenders however, are more comfortable making loans than managing property and would prefer that their borrowers simply keep their loans current. When it becomes evident that the borrower is unable or unwilling to honor the obligation, all any lender wants to do is salvage whatever amount is possible from the collateral.

Foreclosure law is formed and enforced at the state level. For that reason, specific approaches to the problem of allocating rights between lender and borrower vary in each state. However, states fall into one of two categories of legal philosophy. The majority of the states subscribe to the idea that a mortgage establishes a special interest in the property as a lien. In the event of a default on the mortgage obligation, the lender may exercise a claim on the property that is satisfied in court proceedings. Other states provide the lender with rights similar to those of an owner of the property. In these states, the law establishes procedures for the sale of the property in the case of default. In general, lenders in these states are in a stronger position to protect their interests than those in states following the lien philosophy. As a practical matter, the procedures of foreclosure and sale of the property have a similar effect in all states.

At one time, a borrower who was delinquent on a loan payment would have to forfeit all rights to the property, which became the property of the lender. This "strict foreclosure" has been phased out in many states in favor of law that provides the borrower a specified "equity of redemption." This means that the borrower has the right to redeem the property by satisfying the debt. When a lender forecloses a loan, it is this equity of redemption that is being foreclosed, or eliminated. All states provide borrowers with some period of time during which the borrower can avoid losing the property by paying off the loan, but the length of this period varies.

A lender who wants to foreclose petitions the court to cut off this period. In most cases, the borrower is allowed to occupy the property and may even sell it during this period. In some states, the mortgage contract provides that the lender can put the property up for sale in the event of a default; in others, the sale must be conducted under the sanction of the court. This latter procedure is referred to as *judicial foreclosure*. It is a relatively time-consuming and expensive process that virtually guarantees that the lender will be unable to fully satisfy the debt through sale proceeds. However, the purchaser of the property at the foreclosure sale, usually the lender, is assured of receiving a property free and clear of all encumbrances.

Lenders typically acquire the property at foreclosure although they would prefer a sale. Lenders can simply present their lien to acquire the property. Another party could bid more than the unpaid debt, taking the property away from the lender. However, the lender cannot profit from the foreclosure sale. Any excess over the sum of the unpaid debt plus back interest and foreclosure costs goes to the former owner.

22

NONJUDICIAL FORECLOSURE

In many states, the customary mortgage contract is worded to allow the lender to sell the property in the case of foreclosure without going through an extended court process. Such "power of sale" mortgages make it easier for the lender to recover the debt. Though the rights of the owner are not fully protected by the courts, these "nonjudicial" foreclosures are commonly used where state law allows.

In some states (Arizona, California, Colorado, Mississippi, Missouri, Tennessee, Texas, Oregon, Virginia, West Virginia, and the District of Columbia), the predominant type of mortgage used is the deed of trust. This mortgage provides for a trustee who is granted the power to sell the property in the event of default and foreclosure. The trustee must conduct the sale under strict guidelines established in the law of the state. However, the process is straightforward and is more predictable than the alternative of a court-monitored sale. (The disadvantage of not involving the courts is that it may leave the action open to later challenge and scrutiny by the courts. This is rarely the case, however, when the rules are clear and are followed strictly.)

The trustee must provide public notice of the sale. In most jurisdictions there is a certain time and place for the sale, most often the county courthouse on a designated day each month. If you are interested in participating, check periodically with the county clerk for notices of impending sales. Courthouses will have a bulletin board where notice of each property to be foreclosed is posted for several weeks before the sale. However, the notice may provide only a legal description that is adequate to locate the property on a survey map, and not describe its size, features, or condition. You have no right to visit private property just because it has been posted for foreclosure. However, the owners may invite you to visit if your intention is to purchase from them.

Foreclosure destroys all mortgage liens established after the time of the mortgage being foreclosed. Therefore, the buyer receives the property free and clear of the subject mortgage, as well as any mortgages that may have been added later. However, any claims established before the first mortgage was created are still in effect. Any unpaid taxes or charges, as well as any liens placed on the property by a local governmental unit or the IRS, may survive foreclosure as liabilities for the acquiring owner. It is important to have the title searched and to gain the protection provided by title insurance, especially when purchasing foreclosed property.

See Key 25 for a list of states where nonjudicial foreclosure is commonly used.

23

DEED IN LIEU OF FORECLOSURE

All defaults need not result in foreclosure sales. In some cases, a borrower faced with foreclosure may be able to sell the property before losing it. The new owner may be able to assume the old mortgage and bring it up to date. More often, the buyer will arrange new financing and retire the old loan. A distressed owner may have an incentive to sell even though the price is below the mortgage balance owed, since a foreclosure may destroy his or her ability to get another mortgage loan. In many cases, however, the owner cannot afford or is unwilling to sell a home for less than what is owed.

Some borrowers are under the impression that they can merely turn ownership over to the lender and thereby satisfy the debt. During economically depressed periods, it is not uncommon for homeowners to mail in the keys to their homes instead of making up the mortgage payments. However, a lender does not have to accept such a transfer in payment for the debt. There is a good chance that in the ensuing foreclosure sale, the property will not sell for enough to cover the debt plus expenses. In that case, the borrower may still be liable for a deficiency judgment for the difference.

On the other hand, sometimes lenders accept the transfer. Title to the property goes to the lender in a transaction termed *deed in lieu of foreclosure*. When the lender accepts such a deed, the right to a deficiency judgment is waived. In these cases, the lender has determined that possessing the property without delay is preferable to the cost and risk of pursuing both a foreclosure proceeding and a deficiency judgment suit. Often, the borrower is "judgment proof," meaning that he or she has little wealth available to satisfy a judgment, even if the lender is successful in court.

What this means to the buyer seeking foreclosed property is that some homes may become part of a lender's inventory without going through a foreclosure sale. Although you may not have the opportunity to bid at a foreclosure sale on these properties, you may be able to buy from the lender's inventory (see Keys 34–38). One thing you should recognize about such properties is that the deed in lieu of foreclosure process may not resolve all claims against the property. Therefore, when buying from the lender's inventory, it is important to receive a warranty deed to protect against future claims against the property.

24

FORECLOSURE SALES

The result of a foreclosure proceeding is a sale of the property. Money from the sale goes to satisfy the outstanding debt plus accrued interest and expenses. If there is any money remaining, it is used to pay any junior lien holders on the property and, finally, the borrower. If, as often happens, the proceeds are not enough to cover the debt, a deficiency judgment may be brought against the borrower.

The foreclosure sale is conducted as an open auction where anyone interested in the property may enter a bid. Procedures for conducting a sale are set by the courts or within state law and vary from state to state. However, some features are universal. Adequate notice of the time and place of the sale, as well as a description of the property, must be given to both the borrower and the public. This may include an official notice at the county courthouse and some type of advertisement in the local legal newspaper. This is to ensure that the public is notified of the sale and any interested party may bid. Procedures used for entering bids and accepting a winner are written in the law as well.

When a judicial foreclosure is used, the sale is conducted under the instructions and supervision of the courts. In some states, a minimum acceptable price will be set by the court. Some states regulate how much a lender can recover through foreclosure. In all cases, the court must accept the results of the sale before it is finalized. This requirement is to protect the borrower from a large deficiency judgment resulting from too low a sales price.

Nonjudicial foreclosure sales are conducted by the trustee or person designated in the mortgage contract. Procedures are described in the contract and are consistent with state law. There is some potential that nonjudicial sales will be set aside because of a challenge from the borrower. However, most borrowers who feel aggrieved by the sales proceedings will sue for damages rather than set aside the sale. Therefore, as a practical matter, nonjudicial sales are as safe for the successful bidder as judicial sales are.

In most foreclosure sales, the lender is the successful bidder on the property. A lender may bid a specific dollar amount or simply present the debt owed as the bid amount. Outside bidders are encouraged to bid so that the sale is more fair and less likely to be challenged. The winning bidder receives the property in the same legal condition the property was in before making the mortgage. The foreclosed mortgage and any junior mortgages made afterward are eliminated. However, the title may still be clouded by any right of redemption provided to the borrower by state law. This can be a serious drawback to bidders in states that provide a lengthy right of redemption.

An individual investor may feel intimidated bidding against institutions at a foreclosure sale. Most lenders, however, will be pleased to see the property go to an outside party, alleviating them of receiving the property and reselling it. Their primary objective will be to assure that the winning bid is not too low and that they receive what is owed on the mortgage. If you feel confident that the property can be obtained at a good price, bid. You may find it more advantageous, however, to buy from the lender after the foreclosure sale is consummated.

25

FORECLOSURE PROCESS BY STATE

Below appears a summary of what foreclosure buyers can typically expect in each state as they try to identify opportunities to acquire properties noticed for foreclosure. Bear in mind that the legal system in many states provides for both judicial and nonjudicial foreclosures under varying specific circumstances, or depending on the manner in which the loan instrument is drafted with respect to foreclosure rights. It is extremely important for any auction buyer to become familiar with state law concerning foreclosures before attempting to acquire any property. You may do this by simply going to the local library's reference section and reading statutes on state foreclosure law. Alternatively, you can get advice from a real estate attorney. You may also benefit from the advice of a real estate broker or agent or an experienced foreclosure buyer, but you can never completely rely on such advice as factual or current.

An X in the judicial or nonjudicial columns in the chart below indicates that foreclosures are either exclusively or most commonly of one variety or the other. Where both columns are checked, there is estimated to be a 50–50 ratio. The notice period refers to each state's requirement to provide printed advertising notice of a preset foreclosure auction sale date. The process of foreclosure has likely begun well before the advertising notice period. Each state regulates how much notice must be given directly to the borrower before the date of a foreclosure sale. In judicial foreclosures, unless specified in state statutes, it is the court that decides on advertising notice. Once the first notice is issued to the borrower, technically the pre-foreclosure phase has commenced. The public becomes more aware that a property is in pre-foreclosure when advertising notices are published.

Foreclosure auction sales may be overseen by the court, the sheriff's department, or a trustee appointed by the lender. The trustee is typically an attorney who specializes in real estate and foreclosure matters. Any of the above parties may hire a professional auctioneer to conduct the actual sale. Beyond legal requirements, all of the parties above, including the auctioneer, have an interest in advertising foreclosure sales. The more participants, the greater the potential bid. Tracking the notices, mailings, and Internet postings of auctioneers who handle foreclosure sales is another way to learn of pre-foreclosures.

State	Judicial	Nonjudicial	Ad Notice (Days)	Sale By
Alabama		X	21	Trustee
Alaska		X	65	Trustee
Arizona		X	41	Trustee
Arkansas	X	X	30	Trustee
California		X	21	Trustee
Colorado		X	14	Trustee
Connecticut	X		NA	Court
Delaware	X		60–90	Sheriff
District of Columbia	X		18	Trustee
Florida	X		NA	Court
Georgia		X	32	Trustee
Hawaii	X	X	60	Trustee
Idaho		X	45	Trustee
Illinois	X		NA	Court
Indiana	X		120	Sheriff
Iowa	X	X	30	Sheriff
Kansas	X		21	Sheriff
Kentucky	X		NA	Court
Louisiana	X		NA	Sheriff
Maine	X		30	Court
Maryland	X		30	Court
Massachusetts		X	41	Trustee*
Michigan		X	30	Sheriff
Minnesota		X	7	Sheriff
Mississippi		X	30	Trustee
Missouri		X	10	Trustee
Montana	X	X	50	Trustee
Nebraska	X		NA	Sheriff
Nevada		X	80	Trustee

State	Judicial	Nonjudicial	Ad Notice (Days)	Sale By
New Hampshire		X	24	Trustee
New Jersey	X		NA	Sheriff
New Mexico	X		NA	Court
New York	X		NA	Court
North Carolina		X	25	Sheriff
North Dakota	X		NA	Sheriff
Ohio	X		NA	Sheriff
Oklahoma	X		NA	Sheriff
Oregon		X	30	Trustee
Pennsylvania	X		NA	Sheriff
Rhode Island		X	21	Trustee
South Carolina	X		NA	Court
South Dakota	X		23	Sheriff
Tennessee		X	20–25	Trustee
Texas		X	NA	Trustee
Utah		X	NA	Trustee
Vermont	X		NA	Court
Virginia		X	14–28	Trustee
Washington		X	90	Trustee
West Virginia		X	30–60	Trustee
Wisconsin	X		NA	Sheriff
Wyoming		X	25	Sheriff

Source: www.ForeclosureU.com.

* In Massachusetts, the format will appear to prospective bidders as a typical nonjudicial foreclosure process. Foreclosures in this state do actually require the land court's verification that the property is not subject to the protection of the Soldiers' and Sailors' Civil Relief Act.

The source of the information provided above is ForeclosureU.com, a Web site selling products primarily to real estate agents interested in profiting from foreclosure properties. It has been presumed accurate at the time of this writing, but all readers should be cautioned that laws and circumstances change over time. It is again recommended that you research current state statutes concerning foreclosures or that you consult with a real estate attorney or other real estate professional to assure timely understanding of the process in the state where you plan to participate in the foreclosure market.

It is also critically important that you learn whether or not the state in which you are bidding provides the borrower with a redemption period. The right of redemption means that a bidder may win at auction, but a borrower may reclaim the property up to a state-specified period by curing the default with the lender. In more than half of the states borrower redemption after the foreclosure sale is possible. A winning bidder's ability to take title or possession, renovate, rent, or resell must wait until the specified redemption has passed. Where applicable, redemption periods range from 10 to 365 days, and in the case of one state, two years. As of this writing, states providing the right of post-foreclosure sale redemption are Alabama, Alaska, Arizona, Arkansas, California, Colorado, in some cases at court's discretion in Connecticut, Idaho, Illinois, Iowa, Kansas, Kentucky, Maine, in some cases at the court's discretion in Maryland, Michigan, Minnesota, Missouri, New Jersey, New Mexico, North Dakota, Oklahoma, Oregon, South Carolina, South Dakota, Tennessee, Vermont, Wisconsin, and Wyoming. State laws and redemption guidelines are subject to change.

26

BUDGETING FOR YOUR AUCTION BID

Once you have identified a property on which you would like to bid at foreclosure auction, you are going to have to formulate the maximum you may be willing to pay for it. Some would argue that it is important to ascertain what is owed on the property, and possibly increase that amount by lender's costs such as taxes, insurance, legal fees, and so on. The first reason to conduct this research is merely to know if there is enough of a difference between lender's exposure and current or expected future market value to assure that buying at auction is worthwhile. If the numbers are too close, buying at auction may not be the right strategy. The fact is that the attendees at any given auction event will determine the auction value. Planning ahead to put your best foot forward will assure that you do not exceed what is reasonable.

As discussed in "Researching Targeted Properties" (Key 13), another good reason to conduct or to pay to have a title search is to determine what obligations might take precedence over the mortgage being foreclosed. If you are bidding on property where earlier-dated mortgages or mechanic's liens have not been released, you will have to budget to pay off these liens (and any accrued interest) before you can resell the property. If you acquire a property with existing tax liens, municipal liens, or some condo and homeowner association liens, regardless of when they were established, these payoffs must also be budgeted. Property tax and municipal liens, such as water and sewer where applicable, will likely not wait for you to pay them without threatening interest and penalty expenses and possibly selling your property or the rights to it at a tax sale. It is good to clarify with the tax collector what property tax and municipal services might be owed to double-check what you find during title research. Even when a lien of this type is not yet recorded at the registry of deeds, it still must be redeemed. It is good practice to telephone or visit the tax collector's office to obtain this publicly available information before each auction sale. You might also use this contact to learn the amount of current annual taxes. Even if the property is not in arrears, you are going to be obligated for property taxes during whatever period you own it.

If you are fortunate enough to be in a position to pay cash for a property, no doubt you will be pleased to forgo the cost of money, that is, the various costs associated with taking out a mortgage loan to finance your foreclosure acquisition. You may remember the last time you took out a loan. You may have paid points or an origination fee. You almost certainly paid administrative costs, an appraisal fee, and legal expenses. Perhaps you paid for mortgage insurance that covered the lender's interests. All of these "up-front" costs to obtain a mortgage loan must be considered in your expense budget. Then you will have to consider how long you expect to own the property. Monthly payments of principal and interest will lower your total return. Obtaining guidance from a friendly lender may help to minimize costs of financing. For example, an investor who flips property quickly should not take out a loan where points and up-front costs are high. Rolling up-front costs into monthly mortgage payments usually works better. As another example, a flipper may also benefit from taking a home equity loan on a personal residence. Up-front costs can often be minimized, and it certainly alleviates the concern lenders may have when they cannot get an appraiser inside a home that is being foreclosed. Through television advertising or online promotions selling the art of foreclosures, you may have been told how a foreclosing lender may remortgage the property at favorable rates to prevent it from sitting in their real estate owned (REO) portfolio. This may be more likely in negotiation for properties already sitting in REO inventory. It is less likely to be something that a foreclosure bidder can expect. It is advisable to find a lender with whom you can build a rapport. Share your intentions candidly. Lenders will let you know if they are comfortable working with distressed-property scenarios such as foreclosures. Ideally, they will also make recommendations that best suit your financial objectives. Establishing a history of successful transactions with your chosen lender will make future mortgages easier to obtain.

In some states, the transfer of real property is subject to costs for transfer stamps or taxes. Amounts vary, but they are usually calculated as a percentage of the selling or transfer price. In some instances where the transfer taxes are typically split between seller and buyer, it is possible that the foreclosing lender will require the foreclosure bidder to pay both sides of the transfer taxes. This tactic serves the foreclosing lender. It may or may not be verbally disclosed at the auction sale. You are encouraged to review the purchase contract or memorandum of sale before bidding. If applicable, this is where you should find some description of such a variance to the normal sale. This term is not made to be negotiable. The amount can be substantial, so it is important to include it in your bid budgeting.

If you have elected to employ the services of a real estate professional in conjunction with a foreclosure auction acquisition, it is important to have a preestablished understanding of that person's compensation. Although non-foreclosure auctions often invite broker participation, foreclosing lenders usually do not feel the need for it. Some real estate agents with whom you have established a rapport may work with you on a consulting basis in order to get the listing when you turn the property around for resale. Be prepared for the fact that others may negotiate a fee for their advice because a co-broker commission is not likely available. This is a cost that has to be figured into your budget. It is typically paid directly, that is, outside of a closing statement. It pays to be clear about any compensation.

Depending on how closings are arranged in your state, there may be costs associated with transferring the property beyond financing costs and transfer taxes. If you are financing, chances are your lender has already outlined additional costs. If not, be sure to ask. Private mortgage insurance (PMI) is typically required for homes purchased with a down payment of less than 20 percent. It typically costs 2–2½ percent of the amount borrowed, plus an ongoing annual fee of ¼ percent of the loan. If you can afford the 20 percent down payment, go ahead and make it, because PMI is expensive.

If you are not financing, then you may need to fund legal and administrative costs representing your interests. Title insurance may be required. It might also be available at your option. You will need to plan accordingly.

After taking a deed, your greatest expense may be renovating the property to make it suitable for occupancy, rental, or resale. If you have been fortunate enough to gain access to the premises before the auction, you may have some idea of what it is going to take to rehab the house. If you have inspected the house with a contractor, better still. If the property has been well maintained, you may be investing a small amount to make it livable or to reposition the property for resale. On the other hand, because it is rare to have access, you are smarter to overestimate the expenses that may be required. Here is just a small sampling of the items that may require attention but whose condition cannot always be determined until possession: carpeting; wood floors; tile or linoleum; interior paint; exterior paint; drywall; plumbing; heating, ventilation, and air-conditioning (HVAC); kitchen cabinets and appliances; bathroom fixtures; doors; roof; exterior siding; garage; and garage doors. Many foreclosure buyers automatically build in expenses for flooring, paint, and appliances. These are pretty much a given whether you want to occupy the house or stage the property for resale. A smart foreclosure buyer also builds in a contingency amount for the unforeseen. Think about a surprise like having to replace a furnace or a central air-conditioning system. How about water damage or even mold resulting from broken plumbing pipes? Watch out for that septic system surprise. There are thousands of dollars involved in these repairs. It is better to expect the expense and enjoy the additional profit rewards when these budgeted funds do not have to be spent. Not having planned for such expenses, and facing the reality of them, can easily wipe out a profit or even result in a loss.

Once you decide how long you plan to hold the property before reselling it, you must budget for ongoing taxes and utilities. Utility companies can give you a sense of what monthly costs have been over the preceding year. The tax collector can confirm annual taxes for the most recent tax year. Estimating these expenses at a reasonable increase to the preceding year will tell you what to budget. If you are planning to purchase a condominium or a property with a homeowner association, you must also budget ongoing fees for the length of time you expect to own the property. Another ongoing expense consideration is property insurance. A lender will require you to buy property insurance. It is something you will want to do even if there is no mortgage. The policy can be canceled at any time, and the prorated share covering the anticipated period of ownership is your budgeted amount. If the house is to be unoccupied for any length of time, purchasing a policy can be complicated and expensive. It is advisable to check with your own home insurer or someone favorably disposed to working with renovating property to determine costs before you bid at auction. You may find that some insurers will not even consider this kind of risk.

Whereas foreclosure buyers who plan to hold the property for a longer time as occupant or landlord will be less concerned about sales and marketing expenses to resell the property, those who plan to quickly flip ownership may want to figure these costs into their bid budgeting. If you plan to list with a real estate agent or broker, and you don't expect any extraordinary advertising or other marketing activities from your agent, you should face little expense beyond commission, which is also noted below. If you plan to sell the property without the aid of a real estate professional, then you will want to factor in advertising, signs, and open-house expenses among other activities into your pre-bid budget.

No matter what your time frame for ownership, some of the same expenses incurred when you buy a property have to be planned for at time of resale. Unless you plan to sell the property yourself, you must provide for a real estate commission, an agreed-upon percentage of your hoped-for selling price. Even if you sell the property as an FSBO (for sale by owner), you may choose to offer a co-broker commission at the going co-broker share to gain cooperation from real estate professionals. Unless you are capable of and confident in representing yourself at closing, you must also anticipate administrative and legal closing costs. In some states, representing yourself at closing may mean no more than preparing your own deed of transfer, or paying someone else to prepare it. In such cases, it is recommended that you present the deed to buyer's counsel for approval before arriving at closing. There are other states where you may not be able to represent yourself, or you may meet with total disdain from the buyer's attorney. Where the buyer's attorney refuses to cooperate with a nonprofessional, you are going to have to be equally insistent, or you may be compelled to hire your own counsel. Again, where transfer taxes are applicable, you should plan for whatever your dictated share may be. Remember, transfer taxes are going to be calculated at a percentage of a higher resale price in states where transfer stamps or transfer taxes are applicable.

As you can see, anticipating all of the various expenses that can reduce your hoped-for profit can be quite complicated. For the sake of simplicity, an outline summary of each expense consideration appears below.

- Other mortgages and liens of precedence
- Property taxes
- Liens for municipal services
- Some condo or homeowner association liens
- Interest accrued on liens
- Financing costs, including title and private mortgage insurance
- Transfer taxes upon acquisition, where applicable
- Real estate commission or fee upon acquisition
- Closing costs at acquisition
- Renovation/repositioning expenses
- Ongoing taxes and utilities
- Fees to condo or homeowner associations
- Property insurance
- Marketing expenses
- Real estate commission upon resale
- Closing costs upon resale
- Transfer taxes upon resale, where applicable

If you assure that you habitually consider each of these potential expense areas, then the equation to identify your maximum bid actually becomes quite simple:

EVENTUAL RESALE PRICE
minus
ANTICIPATED EXPENSES
minus
REQUIRED MINIMUM PROFIT
equals
MAXIMUM AUCTION BID

Obviously, if you are not forced to bid as much as your predetermined maximum to win the auction, your profit margin offers further upside. There are other considerations. The equation works ideally for investors who intend to flip the property. If you are investing to produce income in a rental property, then consideration should also be given to income potential over the life of your ownership, and the greater potential for longer-term appreciation upon resale. If you are purchasing the property to reside in it personally, then the expense considerations remain relevant. Your required minimum profit may not be as aggressive because you should be able to rely on appreciation over the term of your ownership.

27

WHAT TO EXPECT ON AUCTION DAY

By now it probably goes without saying, but you want to be certain that you know what type of auction you plan to attend. Not all real estate auction ads are created equal. Many auctioneers make a good living by convincing sellers that the best way to market their homes is via auction versus listing with a real estate firm. Auctioneers also market property that is intended to settle an estate and are often hired by attorneys or executors to sell estate property by way of auction. In both of these scenarios there are typically minimum purchase prices that may have been guided by a real estate agent, an appraiser, or another having an opinion. Final bids are subject to executor approval. There may be deals to be had, but these cases do not usually offer the potential for bargain purchases that can be found in foreclosure auctions when lender exposure is well below market value.

To understand the purpose of an advertised auction, it is necessary to read the carefully chosen words in the ad and look for other hints. Foreclosure ads will refer to "foreclosure" or "mortgagee's sale" or "mortgagee's real estate." Legal notices are clear in their intent. Marketing-driven auctions are often less clear, but if you don't find references to "foreclosure" or "mortgagee," you are likely looking at a marketing tactic. Property to be auctioned to settle an estate is usually described as such. A bargain opportunity may be implied, but is rare since an executor usually has a fiduciary responsibility to obtain the highest possible price. Marketing auctions are often held on the weekend and offer previews of the property to increase attendance. Foreclosures are typically midweek, business-hour events, and they rarely afford prospective bidders a peek inside. If you have researched legal notice advertising to precede or to supplement what you find in auctioneer advertising, you can be entirely clear on the intent of the seller.

Be prepared for the possibility of cancellation or postponement. It is always advisable to check with the mortgagee's representative or auctioneer before arriving at an auction sale to assure that the sale is going forward as scheduled. Borrowers may restore their standing with lenders right up until the auction sale is conducted, and in rare cases, even after. It is not unusual to have the auction canceled or postponed at the site and time of the intended sale. Sometimes the auctioneer will get a telephone call adjusting the status of the auction. There are even times when a borrower delivers funds to the lender's agent or auctioneer during the auction sale. There are also circumstances where the lender extends the auction date because the property is being marketed for sale by a real estate agent, or where the lender cancels or postpones after learning that the subject property is under an agreement of sale. Lenders are generally happier to work with the borrower to structure an arrangement that avoids foreclosure.

Once you have completed the basic academic work surrounding auction sales, the best thing you can possibly do to acquaint yourself with the process is to attend auctions without a plan to bid. Auctions may occur at the property being foreclosed, on the courthouse steps, or at a neutral facility like a hotel ballroom. You may attend a single-property auction sale, or a multiple-property sale such as might occur at the courthouse or at a hotel. The sale may be overseen by the court, the sheriff, or an attorney or a trustee. Differences are created by state law and sometimes by the content of the mortgage document. There may or may not be a professional auctioneer conducting the sale bidding. To get a feel for what you can expect and to gain comfort for the day when you show up with a deposit check and the intent to bid, it is very worthwhile to invest time in observing auction sales in the area where you intend to buy.

The more auctions you experience, whether observing or bidding, the more you will come to learn about

1. auctioneers,
2. competing bidders, and
3. bidding.

Auctioneers come in varying types. Professionally licensed real estate auctioneers have different training, styles, and personalities that can affect auction outcomes. Not all conducting these sales are professionally licensed auctioneers. Sheriffs, attorneys, and trustees all orchestrate foreclosure auctions, and they have varying levels of experience and expertise. After the traditional reading of the legal notice by the legal representative or auctioneer, you may be given an opportunity to ask questions, or you may not. There is no guarantee your questions will be answered. There is no guarantee of accuracy in any answers, and there is no warranty for information provided. All of this is to say that consistency is rare unless you have the same auctioneer repeatedly. It doesn't hurt to try to ask a question or two. Some questions you ask might be framed to scare off some of the competing bidders. Asking about property taxes, transfer taxes, or other liens you may already know about can have a paralyzing effect on some competitors. Confirming that the foreclosure sale instrument is a first mortgage or a mortgage of precedence may have some value. You will do well to read all materials made available at the auction, including contract forms. It is important to do your homework in advance so that you are not wondering if you are bidding on a second mortgage or if there are any outstanding property taxes. Study the house you may be bidding on, as recommended in previous keys. You are unlikely to see the inside of it until you buy it. The more auctions you attend, the more confident you will become in reading and understanding auctioneers.

Competing bidders also come in all shapes and sizes. Just about every auction has some complement of nonbidding attendees. They may be curiosity seekers, neighbors, or those studying the process of foreclosure or auction buying. The only attendees generally permitted to ask questions, and the only folks you care about, are those who have come with deposit in hand and are registered to bid. Almost always a small number of people present a deposit, register, and never bid. Perhaps they would step up at giveaway prices. Active bidders are most likely investors, but often include a less experienced auction attendee looking to live in the property that is for sale. A bidder who intends to dwell in the property is a dangerous competitor, because he or she is there to buy the house at a value price, but does not necessarily need the deeper discount required by the investor. Whether a "dweller" or an income property landlord, the patient foreclosure buyer can usually rationalize a higher bid. The foreclosure flipper is focused on the depth of the discount to current market value because he or she does not expect to benefit from appreciation over time. For the flipper, it's all about owning for the shortest time possible and achieving the highest markup possible. Investor types differ by investment horizon and by renovation capability. An investor who has the skills to rehab the property can also afford to pay a bit more than the investor who must pay someone else to perform the work. One further distinguishing investor characteristic is financial capability. The cash buyer has an advantage in that he or she does not incur the costs associated with borrowing. Not that you can recognize cash buyers by how they look, what they wear, or what kind of car they drove to the auction, but this bidder may also be willing to throw up a higher bid. The more auctions you attend, the better you will be able to read and understand the motivation of competing bidders.

Bidding is done by registered bidders who may be given a number, a paddle, or a bid card, or they may not be given any bidding tool. Bids can be made verbally or by physical gesture. Although the auctioneer will call out the progress of the auction, it pays to position yourself where you can see competing bidders. There may be no rhyme or reason to the auctioneer's starting bid point. Some auctioneers ask for a bidder to set the starting point. Some auctioneers work painfully fast, whereas others inch along to squeeze every last nickel from the pool of bidders. Some quickly reveal the lender's minimum bid, and others try not to disclose it unless the minimum has not been met. Bidders may try to control price increments, but ultimately this is in the hands of the auctioneer. Increments often get smaller as the final selling price is approached. Since the auctioneer is duty-bound to fetch the highest price, ample time is usually given to override the most current bid.

It is better to find yourself competing against fewer bidders. Time can be taken to fully absorb the auction environment. Encouraging the auctioneer to reveal the lender's minimum bid is important if the auctioneer is willing to do so before all participating bidders are given a chance. Then at least you will know the minimum for a third party to purchase the property before it reverts to the lender. It is not unusual to find that a bidder is willing to beat the lender bid by a dollar or another modest increment to win the auction. A larger crowd can work itself into a frenzy. The atmosphere can be less clear, and bidding can advance at a faster pace. It is important that you do your homework before arriving at the auction. Know the maximum you should be bidding and stick to it! Getting caught up in the excitement of active bidding can wipe out your planned profit before you realize it. Listen to the cadence of the auctioneer, and pay attention to bidding increments. If bidding is active, you want to be able to place your exact preset maximum bid before giving way to other bidders. The more auctions you attend, the more comfortable you will feel mixing it up with fellow bidders.

Legal notice will specify the deposit required to bid and the additional terms of purchase if you are a successful bidder. Auctioneer advertising may convey similar information. The high bidder at a foreclosure auction surrenders the typically nonrefundable deposit and enters into a commitment to increase the deposit by a certain date and/or close on the purchase in a previously identified time period. Legal notices and auctioneer ads will spell out the amount of the deposit(s) required to bid, and the form in which the funds must be presented. Evidence of the initial deposit will be required in order to register. An agreement of sale, memorandum of sale agreement, or other contract form is executed immediately after the close of bidding. The contract will indicate all obligations of the successful bidder to complete the purchase, including expenses that may not be included in the bid price, such as transfer taxes or fees and some closing costs. It is well worth your time to become familiar with contract terms before bidding. Contract terms do not typically allow for the same financing contingencies that a traditional real estate agreement of sale might. If you fail to obtain financing, your deposit money will be at risk. Therefore, you will need to know how the purchase will be funded before you bid. Controlling anxiety on auction day has everything to do with good preparation and experience!

28

WHAT TO EXPECT AFTER THE AUCTION

Assuming you attended a foreclosure auction, you observed one of three things: the sale was canceled or postponed, the property was sold to a third-party purchaser, or the property was sold back to the lender because no third-party bidder was willing to outbid the lender's bid or minimum.

If the sale was postponed, you should follow up to get the new date on your calendar. It is not at all unusual for a property to go through a number of postponements and/or cancellations before it is actually foreclosed. The frequency of cancellation is high. Some auction buyers consider postponements and foreclosure notices for previously canceled properties to be favorable indicators that the sale is more likely to go forward.

If, at auction, no bidder exceeded the lender's bid or minimum bid threshold, then the property is taken by the lender. The statutes vary greatly by state, but once possession is accomplished, the property is added to the lender's real estate owned (REO) or other real estate owned (OREO) portfolio. Typically a real estate professional is called in to recommend a value and selling strategy for the property. Then it is listed for sale on the open market. It is generally in the lender's best interest to follow this course of action, as the lender should be trying to achieve the highest possible return for its effort. There are times and circumstances where, if a clever buyer acts fast enough to make an offer that meets the lender's needs, the lender may be open to dialogue and negotiation directly with the buyer. These instances are increasingly rare because of the various fiduciary and reporting responsibilities of the lender, but it can be worth the effort when you find a lender willing to deal. The greatest challenges are identifying the individual representative of the lender vested with the authority to sell a repossessed property and then persuading that person to negotiate a sale directly. The vast majority are inclined to turn the property over to a real estate agent or broker. Once a real estate professional is involved, he or she will be duty-bound to guide the seller on the highest possible price, which can be well above the seller's original exposure as lender. The opportunity to achieve the lowest possible price may be lost to the buyer, not just because of guidance on a marketable price, but because the seller's costs will be increased by real estate sales commission and other expenses to transfer the property back out of REO inventory.

Third-party purchasers outbidding the lender must pay the required deposit and execute a purchase or memorandum of sale agreement upon conclusion of the auction. This contract form will contain all other terms required to close the transaction. If the successful auction bidder is unable to close for any reason, or decides not to follow through on or before the contractually committed deadline, the property is likely to be auctioned a second time. In some cases of default by the winning bidder, the second-place auction bidder may be recorded and later approached to step into first position at the price he or she last bid.

Let's discuss what happens if you are the successful auction buyer. First, before bidding you should be aware of whether you are bidding in a state where the right of borrower redemption after the auction sale exists. More details are contained in Key 25, "Foreclosure Process by State," but your ability to take title may be delayed by the state-specified redemption period, ranging anywhere from ten days to one year or more. If the borrower/homeowner cures the default within the redemption period, the property is reclaimed and the winning bidder's opportunity is lost.

In states where judicial foreclosures apply, you may enjoy the benefit of the court system or sheriff's department establishing a date by which the borrower must quit and vacate the premises. If you have won the bidding on a property in a nonjudicial foreclosure and the occupant does not vacate voluntarily, it may be the purchaser's responsibility to remove the former homeowner. This can be an immense challenge in two ways. First, you want to take possession as quickly as possible to rehab the home and prepare it for owner or tenant occupancy or for resale. Second, remember that you have acquired a property in "as is" condition. This means that if damage is done to the premises before you take possession, you own the further-damaged premises with little or no recourse. Needless to say, it is in your interest to move as quickly as possible to establish a workable rapport with the former homeowner. The former homeowner is operating under severely adverse circumstances and is not likely to be friendly. The objective is to approach the former homeowner and current occupant in a manner that achieves the earliest possible departure while assuring a reasonable level of respect for the property.

Closing of the foreclosure sale may occur by mail in some cases. In other cases, you may be required to appear at the office of the seller or appointed representative to convey good funds in exchange for the deed. Although your rights as property owner do not begin until after you have received a foreclosure deed (or other form of property deed), it is really in your interest to notify the borrowers as quickly as possible. In the months leading up to the date of the foreclosure sale, the borrowers are going to feel that they have had nothing but threatening correspondence and communications with their lender, lender's representatives, the court, or the sheriff's department. The sale may have been expected eventually, but the reality is always difficult to accept emotionally. Denial and disbelief are common threads that paralyze some borrowers. Foreclosure is a source of great embarrassment in nearly every case, and the winning bidder is likely to be the next one to communicate with the borrower. Notice that the foreclosure sale was completed will eventually reach the borrower, but probably not in a time frame that meets your needs. If the homeowner is known to be present at the auction, and you sense that establishing contact is possible, it is worth trying to generate a dialogue. If the homeowner is not present, it is recommended that you initiate contact by a letter the same day or by the day after the auction. Otherwise, the homeowner may be wondering what is next. It is important that you identify yourself and offer various means by which you can be contacted: telephone, fax, and/or e-mail. If you are going to try to build a workable rapport, you are going to need to convey that you understand the situation from the homeowners' perspective and evidence your sympathy by expressing a willingness to work with them during this unusual and stressful event. Remember that you are not the party that caused such misfortune, but you can be the one to afford a small degree of dignity if you treat the occupant of such property with courtesy.

It is critical to know your rights as property owner with respect to notices that must be served and eviction time frame. You may invite dialogue in your introductory letter and express a willingness to work with the foreclosed party, but be sure to issue notice(s) to quit and vacate in timely fashion once you take the deed. Obviously, presentation is critical. Do your duty to preserve your rights, but show simultaneous compassion. The former homeowner may opt to simply vacate, which is the best possible outcome. Sometimes the lender's representative may provide you with the keys to the house. Sometimes you may arrange for keys directly from the occupant. There are also scenarios where you may have to hire a locksmith to gain access. If the latter occurs, it will help to have a copy of your deed at hand. If the former homeowner is reluctant to leave, you must consider your options, which may include renting back to the foreclosed party, but only if you think they will be more successful at getting payments to you than they were to a bank or other lender. This is rarely the case. More likely you will have to negotiate a deadline that gives the occupant some reasonable comfort. It is worth waiting a bit longer than you might want if you judge that the house will be treated more respectfully. Sometimes your negotiation might include a modest financial inducement to gain cooperation on both departure deadline and preserving property condition.

If all else fails, again you should acquaint yourself with local eviction statutes. In some states, you may find specific language concerning eviction under circumstances of foreclosure. In other states, eviction guidelines are contained under landlord-tenant law. These options, which include court appearances, may or may not suit your personality. Becoming familiar with the rules will help you decide whether you are going to be comfortable confronting the former homeowner directly or appearing in court. Retaining a good real estate attorney can be of immense value in two significant respects. First, an attorney should know all the rules and may very well have a rapport with the court. Second, the attorney can serve as a buffer or fully insulate you from contact with the former homeowner, if preferable.

29

QUALITY OF THE TITLE RECEIVED AT FORECLOSURE SALES

One reason for hesitation about buying at a foreclosure sale is concern over title to the property. Depending on how the sale is conducted and on state law, the buyer may have a perfectly good deed or may face the possibility of losing the property in a legal dispute. You should check carefully with an attorney and title company, and not buy if there is any doubt of good title.

First of all, recall that foreclosure by the mortgage holder effectively cuts off the rights of the borrower to the property and eliminates the mortgage lien. It also eliminates any subordinate mortgages and most liens created after the subject mortgage (but not tax liens held by local government and vendors' liens that may be held by anyone who worked on the property without being paid in full). If you purchase the property at the foreclosure sale, you obtain the same rights enjoyed by the borrower before the loan was made.

There are several potential limitations to these rights, however. First, do not expect to receive a general warranty deed at the sale. The type of deed you will receive may be called a *foreclosure deed, trustee's deed,* or *special warranty deed*; the name varies from state to state. Whatever it is called, the deed makes no promises about claims arising before the property was foreclosed. Be wary of a quitclaim deed, as it provides no guarantee. In such a deed the grantor gives up whatever rights he or she has, but may not actually have any ownership rights at all.

Second, if the property was not foreclosed under the supervision of the courts, there is a chance that the sale will be challenged and thrown out. This could result from failure to follow the procedures provided in the law or because the winning bid is considered not to be a fair price for the property. As mentioned in Key 24, borrowers who challenge a sale generally seek damages rather than to nullify the sale, so the chances of losing the property are small. In any case, beware of a situation where the winning bid appears ridiculously low.

Anyone bidding at a foreclosure sale should determine that the foreclosed loan represented the only lien. Otherwise, other existing debts carry over to the new property owner.

From the time a mortgage is declared in default to the time it is foreclosed, the borrower has an equitable right of redemption. That means the borrower could prevent the foreclosure sale by paying back the loan plus accrued interest. Once the lender accelerates the loan, the option of merely bringing the payments up to date is lost. In many states, however, the borrower retains the right to redeem the property even after foreclosure and sale of the property. This is called the statutory right of redemption and can vary by state from zero to many months.

The possibility that the borrower could reclaim the property can be a nuisance to anyone who buys at the sale. Although the chances of a previous owner actually redeeming the property are remote, you may have concerns about spending for renovation, repair, and remodeling of the structure. Before bidding at a foreclosure sale, know what kind of right of redemption is provided borrowers in your state. If it is a lengthy period, you may want to avoid foreclosure sales and focus your efforts on properties that have been acquired by lenders, their "real estate owned" (REO) inventory.

30

FORECLOSURE SALES ACQUIRED BY LENDERS

In most states, the lender is allowed to bid on the property at the foreclosure sale. In fact, the lender is often the only serious bidder and ends up with the property. The lender presents the mortgage debt as a bid on the property and obtains it with no additional cash expense. Other bidders must come up with cash or arrange financing for the price of the property. In addition, questions about the quality of the title may discourage outside bidders. In states that provide a lengthy right of redemption, the possibility of the property reverting to a previous owner is an additional deterrent.

The courts recognize the possibility that a foreclosure sale may not yield a fair price and will often attempt to set a minimum price for the property. A price that is too low will make the borrower liable for an unfairly large deficiency judgment. For example, in some states a lender must be prepared to show that the highest bid is a reasonable percentage of the property's market value. This raises the possibility that the sale will be inconclusive if no one is willing to bid the minimum. In most cases, the lender wishes to avoid an inconclusive sale (as well as ward off challenge suits by the borrower) and may offer the minimum to acquire the property.

In today's complex residential financial market, the present lender is not always the entity that originally made the loan. Many home loans are originated (first made) by mortgage banking companies and mortgage brokers. Mortgage bankers package the loans they originate and sell them on what is called the "secondary" mortgage market. This market has grown rapidly in recent years, especially by accommodating lending institutions that kept the loans they originated. The secondary mortgage market (not to be confused with second mortgages) handles trading for the majority of first mortgages, as these are often traded within a few days after origination. Although the mortgage originator continues to service the loan (collect payments and maintain the escrow account), the loan is actually owned by someone else. This may be a private investor that buys loans. In most cases, the loan is one in a large pool of loans held by a specialized secondary market entity. The largest of these entities were created by the federal government, but are privately owned. Fannie Mae holds most of its loans in a large portfolio. Freddie Mac sells portions of its portfolio to investors. Each of these organizations, but especially Fannie Mae, may be the initiator and winning bidder at a foreclosure sale on loans it holds.

You may have heard of Ginnie Mae, nickname for the Government National Mortgage Association (GNMA), though its role in foreclosures is minimal. Ginnie Mae is a government agency that subsidizes loans made to qualified low-income homeowners.

Loans that are insured or guaranteed involve additional entities when they are foreclosed. When a loan is guaranteed by the Federal Housing Administration (FHA) or a private mortgage insurance company, the lender has a claim against the insurer when the borrower defaults. The insurer may pay off the amount of the claim and leave the lender to foreclose. However, often the insurer finds it better to acquire the property and try to recoup losses through resale. The Department of Veterans Affairs (VA), which guarantees loans for qualified veterans, may either pay off the amount of the guarantee or acquire the property. When the property is foreclosed, they may offer a "no-bid," meaning that they pay their guarantee to the mortgage lender, usually serviced by a mortgage banker. That can load up a mortgage banker with unwanted property that may be sold as a forced sale.

Commercial banks are covered by insurance that protects depositors in the event of insolvency by the institution. In many cases, the Federal Deposit Insurance Corporation (FDIC), which is the government agency providing the insurance, acquires the assets of the failing bank, including properties previously repossessed by the institution and nonperforming loans on properties that will soon be foreclosed.

When lenders, companies, and government organizations acquire properties, they place them in special inventories. For lending institutions, this inventory is called *real estate owned* (REO) or *other real estate owned* (OREO). These terms refer to real estate the bank owns other than the property it needs to conduct its banking business.

These organizations attempt to manage the properties to produce whatever income possible, but their intent is to sell them off as expeditiously as possible. They may advertise and take bids, list with professional brokers, or hold auctions. These inventories are the richest source of potential bargain properties available. However, each organization has its own operating procedures and the prospective buyer must be familiar with them. (The procedures of the major holders of REO are described in Key 34.)

31

BIDDING AND FINANCING OVERVIEW FOR A REPOSSESSED HOME

There are various methods used to accept bids and select winners. This Key serves to explain some of the terms used to describe those methods and the financing needed to buy a repossessed home.

A **sealed bid** process requires bidders to submit offers with no knowledge of competing bids. There may or may not be an asking price for the property (in some cases, an acceptable bid must be at or near the asking price). The bid should cover the entire transaction, including any requirement for seller payment of closing costs or seller-provided financing. Usually, such bids are collected over a short period when a listing is first released. This allows adequate time for all interested bidders to respond.

When the bids are opened, they are arranged in order of highest value. If there is a minimum bid price, any bids below the standard are eliminated. If the top bids are identical, the agency will select the winner on the basis of a set of priorities. Generally, cash bids are preferred to ones calling for financing. In some cases, there is a target group (such as someone who will occupy the home) that will receive favorable treatment.

The winning bidder is informed of the results of the selection process and given time to respond. Those who made unsuccessful bids receive their deposits back. A winning bidder who does not respond, will, in most cases, forfeit the deposit, though there are provisions for hardship cases. Procedures for choosing another bid vary. If the winner goes through with the purchase, the deposit is applied to the price.

Open bidding works much like any real estate transaction. The prospective buyer makes an initial offer in response to the seller's announcement of the availability of the property. The seller may accept the offer, reject the offer (cutting off negotiations), or respond with a counteroffer. The counter rejects the terms of the buyer's offer and suggests a new amount. A series of counteroffers from each side may continue until both sides agree or one party cuts off the negotiation. When an agreement is settled, the final contract of sale is signed and a closing date set.

Before placing a bid for property, obtain as much information as is available about the bidding process and any procedures for inspecting the property. Note particularly any restrictions placed on bids and any reservations or priorities set for who can bid. In many cases, bids may be placed through a real estate agent approved by the selling agency. Finally, try to ascertain when the agency will announce the winning bid. You may find it not worthwhile if your bid is tied up in indecision for an extended period.

Financing. Most purchases of real estate require some type of financing. The mortgage lending industry in this country is well developed and is flexible enough to accommodate most borrowers' needs. However, needing a mortgage loan to buy repossessed property can be a problem.

A mortgage loan is secured by the real property purchased with the proceeds. In other words, the lender looks to the value of the property as protection in case the borrower defaults on the loan. That is why the lender requires a property description (survey) and appraisal of the property before approving the loan.

In many situations, if you buy repossessed property you need to have prearranged financing. That is because many sellers do not allow contingencies in the sales contract that would allow buyers to apply for a mortgage loan after the contract is signed. Such a contingency allows you to back out of the agreement and recover your earnest money deposit if the loan is not approved (in fact, most contingencies state the terms of the loan that must be obtained). If you know before bidding that financing will be approved, you can pursue the property with some assurance that a transaction will result and that your deposit will not be lost.

Although a lender will not approve a loan without the collateral specified, it may be possible to get pre-approved based on your financial position. The lender may run a credit check, verify your income and other financial resources, and specify the limit of your borrowing ability. You may even obtain a general description of the quality of property that could be financed through that institution. The lender may rule out condominiums or duplexes, for example. If you need FHA financing, you will want to know any restrictions that apply to the property to be financed. You will have the additional advantage of knowing how big a loan is possible, so you will know the most you can bid for a property.

Another option is to use your present home or some other property you currently own to secure the loan. This option offers the advantage of completely prearranged financing with no risk that the loan on new property will be turned down after you have committed to buy the property. The disadvantage is that you are putting additional property at risk should you be forced to default on the loan. Also, you need to have substantial equity built up in the properties to be able to mortgage them. This type of financing can be expensive, especially if the property already has a mortgage on it.

Seller-provided financing can be an advantage, even when the terms are similar to those available in the market. The financing goes with the sale and, therefore, you won't lose the transaction because financing cannot be arranged. Of course, most sellers who are willing to finance would really prefer cash. So if you are depending on seller financing, you are at a competitive disadvantage to cash bidders.

32

FINDING FORECLOSED HOMES

An investor has three opportunities to purchase a property that has been or is in danger of foreclosure. The first occurs when a homeowner defaults on a mortgage loan and the lender takes action to begin the foreclosure process. A legal notice, referred to as *lis pendens*, is filed in the public record (a notice of default is recorded for nonjudicial foreclosure). Therefore, an investor interested in buying homes in pre-foreclosure may monitor the courthouse records for these notices.

The second opportunity comes at the end of the foreclosure process. If the lender uses judicial foreclosure to recover the debt (determined by the mortgage contract and state law), the property will be auctioned to the highest bidder on the courthouse steps. Although the lender ends up the buyer in the vast majority of cases, anyone may tender a bid at the sale. If the investor submits the winning bid, the property is hers. Public notice is required several weeks before the sale, so that bidders may have time to investigate the property. These notices will be posted at a set place within the courthouse and may be advertised in the local newspapers as well.

Finally, investors can buy properties that have been repossessed by lenders, mortgage investors, and insurers. There is no official public notice when these properties become available, but the selling organizations take it upon themselves to publicize their availability. Some sellers publish lists and booklets of properties and maintain searchable listings on the Internet. Some establish offices or divisions to market the properties. Many sign listing contracts with local real estate agents. A few closely guard their list and make it available only to customers or stockholders.

The point is that the process of finding properties varies depending on which stage of foreclosure you prefer. However, in each case, finding properties requires knowledge of the system and the time and effort to monitor the various notification systems.

Where there is a need to organize information, there is a profit opportunity for those doing the organizing. After all, why should each investor track down this data, when someone could do it once for all of them? Consequently, there are services that monitor *lis pendens* and foreclosure sale notices and collect listings of real estate owned (REO) inventories and make them available to paying customers.

The first such services were a by-product of the record searches conducted by title insurance companies. Although the courthouse records are public information and access is free of charge, finding useful information can be extremely time consuming, as well as confusing for someone without a legal background. Therefore, a service that makes this data more accessible has significant value. In many metropolitan areas, there are specialty legal newspapers that report and list individual foreclosures.

The advent of the Internet makes these services even more valuable. There are a great number of foreclosure information services with Internet presence, as any Web browser search will verify. The following is a briefing of what you might find:

- Some are national in scope, but most are regional or even restricted to one metropolitan area. The local service should be okay if you consider buying only in one area.
- Most include some nonresidential property and undeveloped land along with homes. These can be a good source of income properties.
- The actual listings come in several forms. Some sell annual or monthly printed catalogs that can be ordered over the Internet. Others maintain online databases and can be searched by location and property type and can be accessed by subscribers for an annual or monthly fee. Many of these offer a trial search or temporary complimentary subscription. One service allows you to do a limited search to see if there are any properties in your area. If you find properties, you can get more information by subscribing.

- The bulk of the information concerns REO properties held by lending institutions and government agencies. There usually is a brief description, perhaps an address, and whom to contact if you wish to inspect the property and place a bid. Many also monitor notices of default and fore-closure for those who wish to pursue a pre-foreclosure purchase or bid at foreclosure sales.
- Some sell books and newsletters that provide news and how-to information on foreclosure investing. Many provide a good deal of this type of information for free on their Web site. A particularly informative one is the Real Estate Library, at http://therealestatelibrary.com. Also available are chat groups where investors can exchange information among themselves.

The level of quality varies considerably among the services available. Many of these appear to be very useful for the active investor or even someone looking for a good deal on a home. Unfortunately, some may offer little more than can be found on one's own. Fortunately, in many cases, the cost of trying a service is not high ($30–$40 for a monthly report or one month's subscription). Several provide descriptive information about what is available without requiring payment. For most investors, a bit of investigative work and modest investment is probably warranted. If you are looking to make a one-time purchase of a home for your own use, you might skip these services and contact your local HUD or VA office for a list of homes or authorized real estate agents in your area. (Check out the HUD Web site, http://www.hud.gov, for access to HUD homes as well as links to other government and quasi-government sellers of repossessed homes.) There is no charge for this information.

33

WORKING UP A BID

There are various procedures by which you can make an offer on repossessed property. One method popular with governmental agencies is the sealed bid, whereby you submit an offer with the terms kept secret from other bidders. You bid at an auction, too, but then you know what others are bidding. Quite a bit of inventory can be bid on by making an offer through an agent and negotiating a contract just like any other piece of real estate.

The key to making an offer, regardless of the method, is setting a reservation price and sticking to it. A reservation price is the highest price you will pay for a property without paying more than it is worth to you. If market conditions are in your favor, you should be able to get the property for something less than your reservation price. Your first offer can be for much less than your maximum. The gap between this initial offer and the reservation price provides room to negotiate, if necessary.

Your reservation price is not necessarily market value. Rather, it is the highest price you can pay and still obtain your objective. There may be features of the property that are especially valuable to you, or some that have no value. Therefore, everyone's maximum value is different. In a competitive bidding process, the winner will be the one who values the property highest. It is tempting to pursue a property when bidding starts. Remember, however, that unless the property is priceless to you, winning the bid at too high a price nullifies the whole point of buying repossessed property. After all, you are in this market to obtain a bargain.

To set your reservation price, you must know something about what is available in the current market and, preferably, what sold and for how much. Since you are an active buyer, this should not be too difficult. You may have information on asking prices (maybe even some sales data) for properties that are very similar to the one you are considering buying. Note any differences in the properties that would affect their value to you. If the subject has some important feature that is lacking in the comparison property (appraisers call these *comparables*), add an amount to the asking price. If the subject is deficient in some feature, subtract an amount. How much to add or subtract? If the feature is something that could be added, adjust by the cost of making the addition. If not, you must judge how much you would be willing to pay to have the feature. Ignore items that you would not care about (or, if you will rent out the home, items that would not add to the rent you could charge).

Here is how one successful investor estimates a reservation price:

> I start with my estimate of the anticipated resale price after whatever expenses are deemed necessary to make the property marketable. From the projected, and conservative, selling price, I deduct my estimate of the lender's exposure (including the loan balance, taxes, insurance, and foreclosure costs); my costs of acquisition at foreclosure (transfer taxes); costs of a loan (if any) that I will borrow; renovation costs, including taxes, insurance, and utilities over the anticipated period of ownership; costs of marketing for resale; and costs of ultimate transfer upon sale (transfer taxes). If any money is left after these deductions, then I can consider whether there is enough profit (versus risk exposure) to be an active bidder. There is an occasional exception to estimating the mortgagee's or the lender's exposure or intended bid. There are times during the cycle of real estate investing when the number of foreclosures becomes unusually high. We are in such a period at this writing. Foreclosures are being driven by varying combinations of a challenging economy, unemployment or reduced personal income, increases in interest rates for existing adjustable rate mortgages, risky granting of loans to borrowers who may be challenged to qualify and reductions in home values. The result is that too many nonperforming loans exceed the current market value of the homes being foreclosed. The lenders take them into inventory for resale, but they cannot price properties competitively without taking a loss or writing down the amount of their original loan. Lenders do not want to own residential property, let alone stockpile houses. After extended periods of REO

inventory growth, lenders begin to write down their exposure prior to the auction sale. No two lenders are perfectly alike in their thinking; some will write down much more aggressively than others. There is no formula to estimate lender discounts. Insight can be gathered by attending auctions of properties that fit your desired profile for purchase. You might be able to determine some sense of a given lender's mindset if you repeatedly observe the same foreclosing lender. Another possible means of gaining insight is to identify the area real estate agent or agents who really specialize in working for lenders to list and dispose of REO property. They know which lenders tend to want to move inventory more aggressively, and they often guide the lender on resale pricing. These professionals can be great resources when working on your behalf. Bottom line, you have to attend the auction to know the lender's bottom line. Come prepared to bid. Do your budgeting ahead of time, and hold firm to your maximum bid price. If the lender writes down the value in advance, it only improves your profit opportunity.

Once you have a reservation price, you can devise a bidding strategy. If the procedure is sealed bid with no minimum limit on bid amounts, deduct about 10 percent from your reservation price and submit the amount. The amount of discount depends on how popular you think the property will be. If you have lost several bids previously on similar properties, you might bid your full reservation price. If the seller has set a minimum bid amount, compare it with your reservation price. If it is too high, you might pass and wait for the property to come down in price. In an auction, your reservation price tells you when to stop bidding. Opening bids are usually mandated by the auctioneer.

In a normal negotiation between seller and buyer, you will go through several states of offer and counteroffer. You can offer something substantially lower than your reservation price as an initial offer. Negotiations can continue until the seller agrees to your price or you reach your reservation limit.

If you are seeking seller financing, the terms of the loan should be factored into your maximum price. This can be done by calculating the monthly payments you would pay with market financing at your reservation price. This becomes the maximum monthly cost you would be willing to bear to obtain the property.

34
BUYING FROM LENDING INSTITUTIONS

Savings and loan associations, commercial banks, and even some credit unions make home mortgage loans. Today, many of these loans are sold into the secondary market. However, a sizable proportion are held in portfolio by the lending institution. When defaults occur on these loans, the institution ends up obtaining the property in most instances. The properties are placed in an REO inventory to be managed and resold to the public.

The methods used to sell REO properties may vary with each institution. In fact, one institution may use a variety of methods over time, depending on the size of its inventory and what seems to be working at the time. Some may even consider access to their REO a privilege reserved for account holders.

If the inventory is relatively small, as it is under normal conditions, the institution will probably grant exclusive listings with local real estate brokers. An exclusive listing gives one broker the right to sell the property for a commission to the exclusion of all other brokers. This provides the security necessary to allow the broker to advertise the listing. Other brokers work with the listing broker, when the listing broker belongs to a multiple listing service.

When the inventory is unusually large, it may be worthwhile for the institution to establish an in-house management and sales staff. If a large number of properties are of the same type or are located in the same area, the institution may hold an auction.

Therefore, there are a number of ways to bid on REO property. You may go directly to lending institutions in your area and inquire about currently available homes. You may ask a local broker about homes being sold by lending institutions. (Recognize that a broker's responsibility is to the seller. Ethically, the broker should not disclose details about the seller's need to sell the property. However, the identity of the seller can be disclosed. In fact, brokers will often tell prospective buyers that the owner is an institution that would like to dispose of the property quickly.) Lastly, you may participate in auctions conducted by lending institutions.

In most cases, you will find that institutions act much like any other property seller. There are government-mandated regulations on how they sell properties that can lead to advantages and disadvantages for the buyer.

Advantages. The institution will be relatively anxious to sell the home. The home is probably vacant and not producing any income for the lender. In addition, the lender may have remodeled and repaired the building to make it more presentable. The lender may be willing to make special financing available on the purchase. These factors work in favor of the buyer.

Disadvantages. The biggest disadvantage is that the lender may be slow to respond to offers from potential buyers. There may be some type of administrative committee that must approve sales, especially when the bid is below appraised value. This can be frustrating for the bidder. There also may be a minimum price the lender is determined to get. It may be that the lender is trying to avoid declaring a loss on the loan. A reservation price that is too high may stall the negotiations, although the lender may be able to counter the higher price with favorable financing terms.

The drawbacks do not rule out this avenue to bargain homes. Indeed, lending institution REO inventories are normally one of the best sources of repossessed homes. You will need to understand the ways in which the negotiation can stall and be prepared to offer ways around the problem.

35

BUYING A HUD HOME

The Federal Housing Administration (FHA) provides insurance against default on home mortgage loans. When covered by this insurance, a lender may provide a loan that supplies more than the standard 80 percent of the purchase price of a home. When defaults occur, the FHA often ends up with the home following the foreclosure sale. Because the FHA provides insurance on low-down-payment loans, defaults are more common than on conventional loans. This means that HUD (the Department of Housing and Urban Development, of which the FHA is a division) usually has one of the larger inventories of repossessed homes.

Also known as *HUD homes*, these properties are offered for sale to the public. You may search for available homes in your area by going to the HUD Web page at http//www.hud .gov/homes/ or go through a real estate broker. A list of HUD field offices is on page 191.

Occasionally, HUD will place advertisements in the classified section of local newspapers. (Don't be confused with the reference to HUD rather than the FHA. Whereas the FHA handles the insurance program, HUD is the parent agency that markets and sells the properties.)

Most homes will be offered with an asking price stated. Since there is a limit on the amount of loan that can be covered by FHA insurance, the homes held by HUD will be somewhat modest relative to the market. Homes may include condominiums and even some multifamily buildings. The agency generally does not repair or remodel the properties, except in cases of dangerous situations. If a home is in good enough condition to satisfy FHA standards, a purchase loan on the property may be eligible for insurance coverage. Some homes may include a bonus for fix-up expenses. The FHA does not make loans directly and therefore does not finance the properties it sells.

Once you have inspected the property and decided on an offering price, you may submit a sealed bid to HUD. General procedure calls for holding all bids for the full offer period. When the bids are opened, the highest net offer is accepted. Bidders who will occupy the home are given priority, after which bids from investors are considered.

A bid should state the offering price and any special costs to be incurred by HUD. The agency will pay some of the buyer's closing costs and any brokerage commission on the sale. However, these costs are deducted from the bid price for the purpose of determining the highest net bid to HUD. For example, someone offering $30,000 with no cost to HUD would beat out a bid of $31,000 calling for HUD to pay a commission of $1,500.

The bidding process is straightforward. On the other hand, properties must be examined carefully, for they may be in poor condition. Don't expect a luxury home in the inventory, but you may find some good income property. Finally, HUD provides no financing, but the FHA may provide insurance on a loan you arrange with a lending institution or mortgage banker.

HUD has a special program (Good Neighbor Initiative) whereby people in certain job positions can buy HUD homes at discounted prices. If you are a schoolteacher, a police officer, a firefighter, an emergency technician, or an employee of a nonprofit organization or local government agency, you may be eligible. The discount is substantial—50 percent of the home's appraised value. However, you must commit to making the home your principal residence for at least three years. When you buy the home, HUD makes a "silent second mortgage" for the amount of the discount. After thirty-six months, the lien is released. If you move out or sell the house before the period expires, you will have to pay a portion of the mortgage amount prorated by how long you lived in the home. Also, the homes are in specially designated areas. Generally, homes repossessed by HUD in neighborhoods targeted for revitalization are reserved for the program. For more information, see http://www.hud.gov/offices/hsg/sfh/reo/goodn/main.cfm. For local programs involving HUD homes, see http://www.hud.gov/buying/localbuying.cfm.

36

BUYING FROM THE DEPARTMENT OF VETERANS AFFAIRS

The Department of Veterans Affairs (VA) guarantees home loans for eligible military veterans. When a veteran defaults on the loan, the VA often buys the home in lieu of paying out the amount of the guarantee. When mortgage foreclosures have been frequent in an area, the VA is a good source of foreclosed homes. (Addresses of VA Regional Offices are provided in the Appendix.)

The VA markets homes in a similar fashion to HUD (see Key 35). Bids are accepted from the public (they may be entered through a real estate broker or directly), properties are offered in "as is" condition, bids must be submitted without contingencies, and a five- to ten-day waiting period is used to collect bids. However, there are some important differences.

The VA does not give brokers exclusive contracts to list properties, but it does designate a managing broker to coordinate sales of properties in an area. You may go directly to this broker or work through a broker of your choice. Unlike the FHA, the VA does not deduct the broker's commission from the bid price. However, you must offer the list price for a property unless it is designated for a negotiated price.

Another important distinction is that the VA will finance the homes it sells. These loans are fixed-rate loans at the current VA ceiling interest rate. Down-payment requirements are low, in many cases as low as 5 percent of the price. Furthermore, you do not have to be an eligible veteran to qualify for this financing.

If you have cash or have arranged financing elsewhere, the VA offers discounts for cash bids. Recently, these discounts were as much as 10 percent of the list price. In addition, the VA will pay some of the closing costs for cash bids (this usually consists of paying some or all of the discount points on a loan from a third party). Finally, cash offers are approved more quickly than those calling for seller financing.

Homes held by the VA may be comparable in quality and size to those owned by the FHA. The primary advantage of buying from the VA is the possibility of getting favorable financing with a low down payment. The trade-off is that you may have to bid list price for the home.

Brokers will have a special form on which to submit an offer for a VA home. Preferential treatment is accorded those who will occupy the residence as a home (but investors may also bid), and those who make larger down payments may receive a lower interest rate. Discovering how much the previous owner owed upon default is irrelevant. Once the VA forecloses, a new ball game begins, based on the appraised value of the home the VA gets, as provided by a real estate appraiser.

37

BUYING FROM FANNIE OR FREDDIE

Fannie Mae and Freddie Mac are not government agencies but are related to the federal government. Moreover, both organizations acquire homes through repossession and offer them to the public.

The Federal National Mortgage Association (FNMA), commonly known as Fannie Mae, was created by the federal government to help organize a secondary market in mortgage loans. This means FNMA buys loans that have been originated by others: mortgage bankers, banks, and savings and loan associations. FNMA loans may be kept as investments or sold to investors in "pools." FNMA is a private organization owned by stockholders (though the U.S. government appoints some members to its board of directors). For the most part, FNMA operates as a private business.

Because FNMA owns loans, it often obtains properties when the loans are foreclosed. Like other owners of repossessed homes, the agency markets these properties to the public. The homes in inventory vary in value and quality. There is a limit to the amount of loan FNMA can acquire, but it is much larger than the limit on FHA loans. This means that FNMA will probably have some higher-priced homes than the FHA. Mortgage limits vary with the type of loan and geographic location, and also change over time.

Most of the homes in the FNMA inventory are less than five years old. When necessary, the agency will remodel or repair the homes to make them more salable. However, some are offered "as is."

The agency employs brokers to sell these homes, and they are entered in local Multiple Listing Services. You can search for Fannie Mae homes using the "Fannie Mae-Owned Property

Search" link at the Fannie Mae Web site (http://www.fanniemae.com).

An asking price is set for all properties based on a professional appraisal and an opinion of probable selling price from a local broker. However, the agency is willing to negotiate a price with an interested buyer. In addition, the agency is willing to offer financing when necessary to complete a sale.

There are several advantages to working with FNMA. The agency is relatively free from bureaucratic requirements that slow down negotiations and final approval. It is fairly easy to get information and place a bid. Prices are negotiable and financing is available.

FNMA has less of a social welfare goal than does HUD. Consequently, investors are welcome to bid competitively with potential occupants. Investors may find themselves at a disadvantage in securing as much financing as owner-occupants.

The Federal Home Loan Mortgage Corporation (FHLMC), also known as Freddie Mac, is very similar to Fannie Mae in organization and operation. Freddie Mac offers its homes ready for occupancy, with 5 percent down financing, and no mortgage insurance premiums. (To find a home, check the special Web site established for this purpose: http://www.homesteps.com/. You may register on the Web to have information sent to you when homes become available in your area.)

38

OTHER SOURCES OF FORECLOSED PROPERTY

Other sources of foreclosed property include the following:

- Private mortgage insurance companies
- The Federal Deposit Insurance Corporation (FDIC)
- General Services Administration (GSA)
- Relocation companies

Private mortgage insurance companies. In general, before a lender will make a low-down-payment loan, the loan must either be guaranteed by the VA or be covered by private mortgage (default) insurance. Before the FHA began offering such insurance, there were private companies that served this role. During the housing boom after World War II, private mortgage insurers were relatively inactive compared with the FHA. In recent years, the companies have regained presence in the market, mainly because of the limits placed on the size of loan FHA can insure.

Private mortgage insurance works much like FHA insurance. The main difference is that private insurance covers losses up to only 20 percent of the loan, whereas the FHA generally stands behind the entire loan amount. When a borrower on a loan covered by private insurance defaults, the lender forecloses and takes title at the foreclosure sale. The lender then files a claim with the insurance company for a portion of total losses incurred. The insurance company has the choice of taking title to the property by paying the entire loan or reimbursing the lender by the amount of the claim and letting the lender keep the property.

Because of their limited exposure to loss, private insurers do not take title to as many properties as does the FHA or VA. Nevertheless, these companies may be worth investigating, particularly if there is a headquarters in your area. The oldest, and largest, is the Mortgage Guaranty Insurance Corporation (MGIC). These insurance companies may use a variety of marketing methods and have no rigid procedures for entertaining bids. You may contact the company directly for information, particularly if there have been a large number of foreclosures in the area lately, or look for ads in the paper. Many properties are higher in quality and price than those held by the FHA and VA.

Private mortgage insurers are motivated sellers who know that they lose money by holding vacant property. They have less administrative red tape than government agencies and fewer properties to monitor. Consequently, they may be much easier to deal with and may have property that appeals to your tastes. However, their inventory will be much smaller than that of government agencies.

There is a popular misconception that mortgage insurance serves to protect the life of the borrower. The kind of mortgage insurance referred to here is default insurance, which has nothing to do with life insurance. As the term implies, default insurance is used to insure the lender in the event of a default. The borrower pays the cost, generally when the down payment is under 20 percent. Mortgage default insurance costs vary with the down payment. For a typical 10 percent down payment, the cost is 2 percent of the full amount borrowed at closing, and an annual charge of $\frac{1}{4}$ of 1 percent of the loan, in addition to all interest and principal payments.

Life insurance to the extent of the loan amount is often available to homeowners, and may also be called mortgage insurance, though it is more precisely called mortgage life insurance. Its purpose is to pay off the loan if the breadwinner dies, so the surviving family household members can live debt-free. Often, term insurance is available at a lower cost and will provide the same protection. Nevertheless, the type of mortgage insurance company referred to in this Key offers mortgage default insurance, not life insurance.

The Federal Deposit Insurance Corporation (FDIC) is a government agency created to insure deposit accounts at commercial banks. You probably have seen signs at your local bank advertising this coverage. When a bank fails, the FDIC moves in and either arranges a merger with a healthy bank or closes down the institution and takes over the bank. In either case, the FDIC obtains the assets of the failed institution (in merger cases, the FDIC may take assets the merging bank does not want). These assets include any REO held by the bank.

The FDIC generally markets properties through exclusive listings with local brokers. In addition, regional offices have sales staffs that will receive sealed bids for properties. From time to time, there may be auctions when enough properties exist to make one feasible. Prices and terms are negotiable. The FDIC can provide seller financing, if necessary. These interim loans have terms of three to five years with a long-term amortization schedule and a balloon payment requirement. For more information, see your broker or the closest sales office of FDIC. It will be listed in your phone directory under "Federal Deposit Insurance Corporation." Some directories print government agencies on colored paper in the front or rear of the book. If there is no listing in your local directory, try the nearest major city. Information is also available at http://www.fdic.gov/buying/index.htm.

As the FDIC's inventory diminishes, there may be a policy change that will shift their inventory to another agency, or a plan to dispose of it themselves more quickly. Such a change could create brief but excellent opportunities for bargain hunters. Stay in touch with real estate publications and people in the real estate market to be informed of possible changes, not only for a change in FDIC policy, but for any matter.

General Services Administration. The GSA manages property owned by the federal government and used in its operations. On occasion, the agency disposes of some of these properties as well as any properties seized by the government during law enforcement operations. Sometimes these properties include single-family homes. The agency uses auctions and sealed bids to liquidate the properties. The agency publishes an IFB or "invitation for bids" on each property. To submit a bid, you need to include a seed deposit of around 10 percent of the bid price. If your bid is accepted, you will receive a quitclaim deed to the property. To receive a newsletter that keeps you apprised of available properties, go to http://propertydisposal.gsa.gov/Property/About/Awards.asp.

Relocation companies. Homes held by relocation companies are not foreclosed homes, but offer opportunities to negotiate good bargains with highly motivated sellers. Furthermore, the fact that a relocation company is trying to sell a home, rather than its resident-owner, usually means that a buyers' market exists, and good prices should result.

Companies with offices or other facilities around the country periodically need to transfer employees from one location to another. This is particularly true of executive and technical personnel. Often these employees buy homes even though they are aware of the possibilities of frequent relocation. When market conditions are good, selling these homes is no problem and often is an additional source of income for the homeowner. In slow markets, however, an employee may not be able to sell quickly without taking a sizable loss. Many companies assist employees by reimbursing losses or buying the home from the employee. There are firms that specialize in marketing these homes, and they are often referred to as *relocation companies*.

When a relocation company takes over a home, it will usually refurbish the property, if needed, to make it more appealing to buyers. This generally means new carpet and a coat of paint. The property is put back on the market by listing it with a broker. Therefore, the way to find such homes is by contacting a broker who is a member of the local Multiple Listing Service (the MLS is a system that allows any member broker to sell any home in the system). Brokers frequently hang a "Relocation Company" sign on the "For Sale" sign to make the buyer's motivation obvious to the market. It will also signal a message that the house is ready to be moved into, so there need not be any negotiation on the date of possession.

In most aspects, buying a home from a relocation company is just like buying from any other seller. However, the company may be more flexible, since the home is vacant and is costing the company money to hold. In most cases, the company should be amenable to reasonable offers. Do not expect to bargain for seller financing. On the other hand, the company may be willing to pay some closing costs. In addition, you will be able to include contingencies in the contract for financing, inspections, and other considerations. This is usually not possible when bidding on fore-closed homes.

Don't expect to buy one of these homes at a rock-bottom price. In most cases, these are quality homes and should command decent prices in all but completely devastated markets. Do expect to find a motivated seller who will work with you to try to reach an agreement.

39

SELLER DISCLOSURE AND "AS IS" SALES

In most housing transactions you have some recourse to the seller for failing to disclose certain defects. Often this is not meaningful because sellers move away and are difficult to reach or have so few assets that it is not worthwhile to pursue them. Still, if a seller or a broker has failed to disclose a defect or lied about it, you may be able to hold the individual responsible—unless that person sold the house "as is."

In many states, there are disclosure requirements for structural defects, termite infestation, lead-based paint, underground storage tanks, asbestos, and other conditions. A seller is obligated to inform you of these known hazards. If the property is offered "as is," however, you accept it in its present condition, whatever that may be. The words *as is* should set off an alarm that something may be wrong. Be certain to have a professional inspector check out the problem very carefully (but be aware that the standard inspection performed before closing covers only *visible* defects; an inspector generally is not responsible for structural problems that are covered by wallboard, carpet, or other components of the house).

The "as is" clause may not protect the seller from failure to disclose latent or hidden defects. For example, suppose there had been a serious fire, the damage from which was completely concealed. The buyer could not detect such on inspection, so the "as is" provision might not protect the seller because the defect was hidden. A seller must disclose this even when selling "as is." You should know that this disclosure requirement does not apply when buying property from a lending institution. Unless some type of warranty is explicitly provided, you should not assume the property is in habitable condition until thoroughly inspected.

111

It is generally a good idea to perform your inspections well in advance of closing, whether or not the property is offered "as is." When it is sold "as is," be especially wary of its condition. Include in your purchase contract a statement giving you the right to various inspections, with enough time to perform them, such as ten business days after the acceptance of the sales or purchase contract, whatever the agreement is called.

How about "stigmatized" properties? These are homes where some gruesome crime was committed, a well-known suicide occurred, or the previous owner died of some dreaded disease. In short, the property comes with a handicap because many people would feel uncomfortable spending any time in the house. The problem here is that there is no way to "fix" the problem. Only time will obliterate the stigma. Unless you plan to demolish the structure or change the use considerably, such properties should not be considered. Of course, if you plan to live there a long time and don't mind being the neighborhood "weirdo," then you probably will get a good deal.

40

THE INSPECTION

It is common practice to do a walk-through inspection and hire a professional inspector before buying a home. Such due diligence is even more compelling when buying a property that is offered for sale at a below-market price. By its nature, such a home has some drawback that reduces its market appeal. It is the investor's task to find out what that is and assess the remedy.

Much can be accomplished with a cursory examination of the property, even if you are not highly knowledgeable about construction techniques and quality. You probably will not want to have every property under consideration professionally inspected. (In some cases, you may not be allowed to enter the home for an inspection though you can discern much by visiting the property.) Instead, you will need some type of winnowing process to eliminate the ones that do not fit your strategy. Let the pros look at the ones that appear acceptable to the untrained eye.

How you evaluate a property depends on, first, whether you will live in the home or use it for income production, and second, how much you can afford to invest in turning the property around. If you are looking for a personal residence, you will look at the property primarily from the standpoint of your personal preferences and needs. If the home has some unique quality that you value, you may go to greater lengths to correct the things you do not like. On the other hand, if the property will be rented out or sold back into the market, your objective is to make it safe (compliant with local codes) and attractive to the typical end-user. Likewise, if the property is selling for a large discount compared with similar homes in market-ready condition, you can afford to do more drastic rehabilitation.

At the first examination of the property, try to detect the existence of flaws that are basically *incurable*. These are things that cannot be changed in any practical sense, yet have a detrimental effect on the property's value. If the property has any of these problems, it should be rejected unless the price is extremely low:

- Noisy, crime-ridden, and disruptive neighborhood (unless there is an active and substantial renovation movement ongoing and you think it will turn the area around).
- A neighborhood that is in transition away from residential (unless you are buying the property for the land and plan to change the use).
- Area where surrounding homes are not maintained.
- An awkward floor plan. Think about the routine functions around the home and how they would be accomplished with this layout.
- Structural type. A large home with several stories will not be as popular as a one-story house of the same size. However, in some locations, a two-story house that provides a small garden or yard may be preferable to one that consumes the whole site.
- Lack of site size or awkward orientation on the site. Unless you can buy surrounding land parcels, you cannot change this situation.

Next, look for things that can be changed or corrected, but require substantial expense to do so. These flaws are not necessarily fatal, but might eliminate any property except the most deeply discounted homes. One problem with taking on these types of properties is the difficulty of fully assessing the cost of repairs. Indeed, many of these problems can be much worse than they first appear. In general, problems in the following areas should eliminate all but the lowest-priced properties:

- Drainage (may require extensive landscaping and underground channeling; may be hard to find a spot where excess water can drain to; may have already caused extensive structural damage).
- Water leaks (can be hard to stop; may indicate drainage or guttering problems; may indicate more serious structural damage).
- Inadequate electrical service (may require extensive rewiring; may coincide with inadequate outlets and lighting for modern usage).

- Foundation damage (hard to tell how extensive without tearing into house; need to fix cause as well as damage).
- Ventilation (may be caused by orientation of house relative to prevailing winds; may require new windows; places undue burden on heating and air-conditioning equipment).
- Hazards such as lead paint, asbestos ceilings and insulation, and radon (detection may require special tests; may not be too much of a problem but could complicate resale if not eliminated; elimination often costly).
- Lack of trees (it takes a long time to cultivate trees from saplings and mature trees are expensive and do not transplant easily).

Finally, there may be items that need attention and will not cost a significant sum, yet fall within the category of things that normally must be replaced at some point in most homes. Therefore, the existence of these problems should be noted and used in negotiating a price, but should not eliminate the house from consideration:

- Worn roof covering (if not leaking; a leaky roof requires closer examination of roof and attic structure).
- Outdated or faulty bath and kitchen fixtures and equipment (minor remodeling of these rooms is one of the most cost-efficient upgrades available).
- Unattractive or worn-out paint and floor coverings (relatively minor investment here can make a big difference in appeal).
- Broken windows and doors.
- Outmoded or cheap hardware (installing better doorknobs and light fixtures can improve market appeal).
- Old, undersized, or inefficient heating and air-conditioning equipment (expensive but can improve comfort while lowering operating expenses).
- Dead lawn and lack of landscaping.

Price out solutions to any of these problems that are apparent and factor that estimate into your offer. The seller may not agree that these are problems. That is the signal to find another property.

41

CONTRACT OR SWEAT EQUITY?

One way to buy a house at an attractive price is to take on the responsibility of a property that needs repair or remodeling or both. Unfortunately, paying someone to fix up the property may negate any reduction in price you were able to negotiate. Traditionally, people with more time than money have been attracted to the "handyman's special" because they could invest "sweat equity" (time and the willingness to spend it making improvements and repairs) to bring the property up to some acceptable standard of quality and condition. However, there is a limit to what the layman should undertake. Some repairs require specialized equipment and knowledge and, if not done properly, can render the property even less appealing and possibly even dangerous.

Knowing what you can accomplish using your own efforts is important to two decisions. First, whether you do the work yourself or contract it out may affect how much you offer for the property. If the work requires professional attention, you may need a larger discount to make the deal work. Second, if you decide to buy the home, knowing how much work will need to be done professionally will help you put together a rehab plan.

Here are the major factors you should consider when making your evaluation:

Time. Do you plan to do the work in the spare time left over from a job and other life responsibilities? Do you plan to live on the property while completing the work? If free time is limited or there are things that must be completed quickly to make the property habitable, you may need to use some hired help. Unless you are experienced in the building trades, many of these tasks will take longer than anticipated. And there is always the possibility of finding bigger problems in the course of making a repair.

Knowledge and skill. If you must learn how to do each task, the work will take more time and the results may not be totally satisfactory. For some people, this is fine. They use the first house they tackle as a learning experience and are content to live with, or take the time to fix, their mistakes. If you are more critical, you may want to avoid doing anything that shows. In general, if the property will be used by tenants, your first concern should be durability. If it is for personal use, your first concern may be appearance and convenience. If you have time, but knowledge is limited, you may be able to work out an arrangement with a professional contractor under which you do much of the preparation work, tearing out the old material and cleaning up the site, for example, before the professionals come in and complete the job. That could save quite a bit of costs and still result in a high-quality rehab. Be aware that many remodeling and rehabilitation jobs require building code permits and inspections. In many cases, the regulations require that licensed tradesmen do the work.

Temperament. Some people do not mind plodding along on a long-term project, content with the gradual progress being made. Others like to get into the heat of the battle and complete a job while the juices are flowing. Many of the tasks required to rehab a property are of the long-term type, especially when you are doing them yourself. Of course, bringing in teams of professionals will speed up the work. The slow approach gives you time to evaluate the effect of the change and to decide on how you want it done. The quick approach requires you to decide much of this beforehand, and any changes in midstream must be decided without much deliberation.

Financing. Obviously, how you finance the work is critical as well. The term *sweat equity* implies very little in the way of cash expense, but that is misleading. Even for do-it-yourselfers, there will be considerable costs for materials, tools, and possibly government permits. If you have the luxury of time, these costs may be met through periodic use of available cash, a tax refund, or a bonus here and there. If the job must be done on schedule, there probably will be a need for some financing to make sure materials are available when needed. Financing imposes a cost of its own and affects scheduling, because the costs increase as the project is drawn out.

There are a number of ways to finance rehab. Self-financing can be done in conjunction with the gradual improvement approach. Unsecured loans, even credit card debt, can be used for small to moderate expenses. A home improvement loan, in the form of a second mortgage, could be used. These types of loans tend to be expensive, so that there is a strong incentive to repay them as soon as possible. It could be possible to refinance the house after rehab at a higher loan amount to retire both the original purchase mortgage and the improvement loan. Ideally, your efforts at rehab will raise the market value of the home enough to support the larger loan. A home equity loan might be used, but this option probably will not be available unless you have significant equity in the property. In other words, if you purchased with a low-down-payment loan, you will not have sufficient equity to get much of a home equity loan. However, if it is feasible, such loans carry interest rates not much higher than first mortgages. There probably would be no need to refinance. For certain borrowers, there are loans that can be used for both purchase and rehab. If you are eligible, this may be your best choice. More detail is provided in the next Key.

42

FINANCING PURCHASE AND REHABILITATION

Buying a house that needs substantial work can provide a bargain, but financing the venture may be tricky. A conventional lender will base the loan on the current value of the property. To finance the rehab work, you will need to get a home improvement loan or a nonmortgage loan (if you do the work yourself, you may be able to buy materials with a credit card), then refinance the first mortgage when the work is completed. Ideally, the house will appraise high enough so that the new loan will cover the rehab expenses.

If you don't mind doing some paperwork, there may be a better way. The Federal Housing Administration (FHA), a part of the Department of Housing and Urban Development, has a program that makes available special loans that combine purchase and rehab. With one of these loans, you can buy a home with a mortgage based on the house's value *after* rehab is complete. You do have to comply with a set of requirements and submit cost estimates and plans to the FHA, but the result can save the expense of getting high-cost home improvement financing and of refinancing the first mortgage later.

The FHA doesn't make loans, but insures private lenders who make the loans. If the borrower defaults, the FHA will step in to reimburse the lender's costs of foreclosing the loan. The most popular insurance program is the 203(b) program, which insures low-down-payment loans on modestly priced homes. The rehab program, 203(k), works the same way, except that the loan includes rehab and remodeling expenses. The loans are made by private lenders, approved by the FHA to do this kind of business. (For information about the program and a list of approved lenders, go to the HUD Web page, http://www.hud.gov/offices/hsg/sfh/203k/203kabou.cfm).

The 203(k) program is intended for single-family homes. However, the FHA includes homes with one to four units in that category. In fact, the agency is somewhat broad in what qualifies, including the following:

- Up to four dwelling units, as long as they are attached. No separate apartment in the backyard.
- A demolished building, as long as some of the foundation is used in reconstruction.
- Conversion of one big house into up to four units or conversion of a multi-unit building into a single-family structure.
- Purchase of a house and separate land and moving the house to the land.
- A residential property with a limited amount of nonresidential space. However, the loan will pay only for work on the residential parts of the property.
- Up to four condominium units, as long as they are in one structure. Town houses also qualify if they are separated by effective firewalls. Special requirements apply to condominium properties. In addition, the borrower must occupy one of the units.

Using the loan to buy and rehab a property is only one way it can be used. You can use it to buy a property and a house on another site and to pay for moving the house and setting it on a foundation on the purchased property. Further, you can use the loan to refinance an existing mortgage on a home you own that needs rehabilitation.

Here's what the FHA requires:

- The home is a one- to four-unit structure.
- The home is at least one year old.
- The property must conform to local zoning ordinances.
- Rehab work must cost at least $5,000.
- Eligible rehab work includes repair of existing structures, additions to the structure such as added rooms or a garage, updating of obsolete space and equipment, and remodeling. The agency is especially receptive to improvements that eliminate health and safety hazards.

- Cosmetic and minor repairs may be covered but only if they are in excess of the minimum $5,000 amount allocated to major rehab work.
- All new and remodeled spaces must conform to stated energy conservation standards. For example, adequate weatherproofing must be part of the work. Also, any replacement equipment must be energy-efficient.

Here is how the program works. When a contract to purchase (in the case of purchase and rehab) has been signed, you find an approved FHA 203(k) lender and make an application. In addition to the usual loan application, the lender will require documents describing the work that will done and how much it will cost. As part of loan processing, the lender may commission an "as is" appraisal to estimate what the property is worth before rehab. A value-after-rehabilitation appraisal will be made as well. The loan amount is based on the lesser of the "as is" value plus costs of rehab and 110 percent of the value after rehabilitation estimate. When the loan is approved, a special escrow account is established containing the proceeds of the loan earmarked for rehab. This account can be drawn upon as the work progresses. The FHA requires inspections along the way before these draws can be made. Also, 10 percent of each draw is held back to make sure no workmen's liens are placed on the property.

All this oversight and deliberation may not seem appealing. And for some, it may prove too cumbersome and limited to work. However, the program is intended to result in a quality addition to the housing stock and to help energetic people get into a home of their own. If you feel that working with such a program will not jeopardize your plans, the FHA 203(k) program may be just the ticket.

43

LOCAL GOVERNMENT RESTRICTIONS

If you plan to physically change the property that you acquire, you will undoubtedly confront several local government laws that affect how you proceed. Although in some locations, such laws are not in effect or are not diligently enforced, many localities take these matters very seriously, and failure to comply can lead to additional expense, delay, and even criminal penalties. In fact, it is best to become familiar with local requirements before committing to a particular property.

Local governments do not pass such laws merely to harass citizens who want to improve their property. The laws serve the purpose of trying to assure that structures do not pose threats to public health and safety and that land uses that might interfere with one another are not in close proximity. Blanket restrictions, as well as private covenants placed in property deeds, help to make an area more compatible to residential use. And whereas everyone may have a different concept of a pleasant residential setting, the law must establish one standard for all. That is why the standards exist as minimum requirements. Anything over the minimum is left to individual taste or private covenant.

For renovation work, two types of local restrictions are most important: zoning and building codes. Zoning affects how a property is used. It is intended to keep incompatible uses separated. It comes into play if you want to change the use of the property, such as convert a single-family home into a duplex. It may also be relevant if you want to enlarge a structure or build additional structures on the lot. Building codes are used to prevent substandard construction. You may need to comply with building codes if you construct something new or rebuild, enlarge, or remodel an existing structure.

Zoning. The zoning ordinance affects how properties are used. In many cases, this refers not only to the type of activities (residential, commercial, industrial) but also to the intensity of use. In other words, the ordinances may have established specific zones where homes may be built on quarter-acre lots, whereas other zones may require two-acre lots for homes. Apartment buildings will be permitted only in zones with different density restrictions. Consequently, you may need to apply for rezoning if you do one of the following:

- Enlarge a house by adding rooms or increasing its height. Most zoning ordinances have setback, side yard, and height restrictions.
- Convert a single-family to a multi-family home. You may also need authorization to go the opposite way; converting a multifamily structure to a single-family home.
- Use a single-family home for group housing or as a day-care center.
- Convert a house to commercial uses, such as a hair salon or a tax preparation service.

It is also a good idea to check the zoning map to determine whether the current use is in conformance. When a zoning ordinance is passed or revised, some existing uses may not conform to the law. These property owners are given time to remove the "nonconforming" uses. In most cases, these uses can remain but cannot be substantially rehabilitated or reconstructed. If you buy a nonconforming use, you may have a surprise when it comes time to apply for a permit.

Zoning is exercised by municipal governments but may also apply to areas within a mile or so of the city limits. In some states, cities have "extra-jurisdictional territory" authority that extends beyond the city boundaries. All the area under the city's control is classified by a particular "zone" that lists the types of uses and densities allowed in that zone. The city planning office maintains a map showing the location of these zones. The zoning ordinance defines permitted uses in each zone.

If what you want to do with the property does not comply with the current classification, you can appeal to the city to change the classification. This is called a *rezoning request,* and you apply for it at the city clerk's office. These applications are reviewed by the planning department and the planning and zoning commission. The commission and the city council will hold public hearings to allow citizens to object to or support your proposal. The city council then approves or rejects your request. If you cannot get rezoning, you may be able to get a variance or a special-use permit. You have to show that the current restriction makes it impossible or impractical to use your property.

Some zoning ordinances establish a hierarchy of land uses, with the least intensive at the top and the most intensive at the bottom. For each zone, a use that is higher in the hierarchy than the use allowed is also allowed. So, for example, you would not need a rezoning to convert a duplex into a single-family home, as long as the duplex is a conforming use. The ordinances are called *cumulative* and are in contrast to *exclusive* zoning, which allows only the uses proscribed in the ordinance for each zone.

Building permits. Any type of construction or significant remodeling will require a building permit. Like zoning, these permits are primarily a function of municipalities, but in some states, counties may be authorized as well. Contact the building inspector's office in the city where the property is located to get information on requirements and application procedures.

In general, here is how building permits work. Before construction or remodeling, you would take a plan showing all the work that will be done and file an application at the building inspection office. There will be a nominal fee, depending on how much work will be done. The office will check to see whether the proposed structure is in compliance with the zoning ordinance and other laws. The city will have a set of construction standards to which the work must conform. For example, the building code may require wall studs at 18-inch intervals or so many electrical outlets per room or the installation of drain cleanouts in the plumbing system.

There will be a series of inspections that apply to new construction. For remodeling, only the systems being worked on need be inspected. Any failure to pass an inspection requires the owner to bring the work into compliance. When all inspections have been successfully completed, the owner can apply for a "certificate of occupancy" that states that the structure may be safely occupied.

Other permits. There may be other permits that affect your plans for reconstruction or rehabilitation:

- Demolition permit. Cities often require a permit to take down a structure. Basically, this is required to assure that utilities have been shut off before demolition.
- Driveway permits. Some cities require a permit to build or rebuild a driveway or walkway abutting the street. The usual safety concerns apply.
- Moving permit. A permit may be required for moving a structure on the public roads. Along with the permit comes assistance in selecting the best route.

If you anticipate that a property will require more than cosmetic remodeling, you should find out as much as possible about how local laws will affect your plans. Many cities have prepared convenient brochures and booklets explaining local development laws and whom to contact. You may also have luck finding information on the Internet by accessing the city government Web site.

In addition to local restrictions, you should check into regulations enforced by state and federal governments. In particular, look into wetlands regulations (see http://www.wetlands.com/regs/tipge00a.htm) and the Americans with Disabilities Act (http://www.usdoj.gov/crt/ada/adahom1.htm).

44

SPECIAL PROGRAMS FOR QUALIFIED HOMEBUYERS

Local, state, and federal governments have expressed concern over two related problems: the decline of inner-city neighborhoods and the lack of affordable housing. Often the two concerns coincide in special programs aimed at helping people buy homes or improve the homes they own in depressed areas of the city. If you qualify for one of these programs or if you are willing to live in an area pinpointed by the city, you may be able to acquire a good home for low cost.

These programs have a variety of things to offer. Some actually provide houses at low prices. Others provide special financing with below-market interest rates and favorable terms. A few promise to lower other homeownership costs, such as property taxes. All of these programs are focused and administered largely at the local level. Therefore, they may not be available in your area and, when available, may have features quite different from those in other areas. Here we provide a general overview of the types of programs you may encounter and show how to find out more.

Urban homesteading. Do you recall reading about the homesteading programs that settled the American West? Anyone willing to carve out and work a farm in the new territory could claim the land for free or a nominal amount. Some cities have similar programs for anyone willing to live in specific parts of the city. The city deeds over the home for a nominal amount to an individual for use as his/her home. The homes usually have been acquired by the city for back taxes and may require repair and rehabilitation. There may be, as well, restrictions on who can acquire the homes. The "buyer" may be required to bring the home up to code standards and live in the home for a specified period. Additionally, there may be some restrictions on resale. If interested, check with the mayor's or city manager's office in the locality for program availability.

Mortgage revenue bond programs. More ubiquitous than homesteading is the mortgage revenue bond program that provides special financing for first-time homebuyers. Bargain financing is the next best thing to a bargain price on the house. And you may be able to get both, if the home is in an area targeted for renewal by the city. The mortgage bond program provides special mortgage loans at interest rates significantly below the going rate in the market. The loans are offered by local lending institutions (banks, savings and loans, mortgage bankers) who sell the loans to a local or state housing finance agency. The agency raises funds by issuing municipal bonds. Because these bonds are exempt from federal income taxation, the agencies can borrow at rates lower than those available to private mortgage lenders. The low rate is passed on to the borrower.

The catch is that the borrower must fit certain characteristics, including not having owned a home for the past three years. There may be income and house price limits that vary by locality. If you fit this description, you can buy a home anywhere in the jurisdiction. If not, you still may be able to get a loan if willing to buy a home in areas targeted by the city, usually in inner-city neighborhoods. In some cases, investors are allowed to participate when buying homes in the target areas.

Some areas have programs that provide assistance for down payments and closing costs that work in conjunction with the mortgage bond program. Usually, these are restricted to the lowest income categories eligible for assistance. To find out more about program availability, contact the housing finance agency for the locality or, as often is the case outside the largest cities, the state housing finance agency. Information on loan availability may be had, as well, from local lenders participating in the program.

Mortgage credit certificates. This program is an alternative to the mortgage revenue bond program and operates with the same qualifications and requirements. The difference is in the form of assistance provided. Instead of a below-market interest rate, the homebuyer receives, from a state or local government, a certificate that allows the buyer to claim a credit on federal income taxes each year. The certificate credit rate varies depending on the issuer, but the permissible range is from 10 percent to 50 percent. The credit the homeowner may claim equals the credit rate times the amount of interest paid on the loan. If the credit rate exceeds 20 percent, the annual tax credit may not exceed $2,000. A tax credit reduces the **tax bill** dollar for dollar, so the certificate could mean up to $2,000 in cash assistance each year for the homebuyer.

Affordable housing programs. During the 1990s, the federal government and a number of local governments created programs to improve access to housing for those with below-median incomes. The ingredients in these programs vary greatly: production of low-cost housing, rent subsidies, special financing, cash assistance to buyers, and technical assistance for those who need to repair their homes. Often, the programs are coordinated through a local office of affordable housing or some similar title. Check locally to find out availability and requirements.

There are a number of efforts conducted by nongovernmental groups, generally nonprofit altruistic or religious organizations devoted to affordable housing or inner-city renewal. Of note is the program run by Habitat for Humanity. The organization builds new homes with volunteer labor and donated materials for those who qualify. Beneficiaries are required to contribute to the construction effort. There often is special financing to make the home even more affordable.

Enterprise zones. Another effort to stimulate economic activity in depressed areas is a program that applies special rules to those areas. For the type of activities desired, the city may relax regulatory requirements, waive normally required fees, and provide property tax breaks. The activities usually are oriented toward employers and businesses, but homebuyers may come in for special treatment under some programs. Check with the city administration.

45

NON-FORECLOSURE AUCTIONS

When markets are slow and foreclosures abound, inevitably there will be a number of large real estate auctions. Holders of REO periodically turn to auctions to help clear their inventories, and individual owners may use the method to move properties that are hard to sell through more traditional means. The auction process is a good way to attract a number of willing buyers and to assure sales of properties.

Should you, as an individual investor or homebuyer, participate in this process? You may think that bidding at an auction is for professionals who are savvy to the ways of auctioneers and that a novice may get lost in the flurry of activity at a typical bidding session. To some extent this is true. You do need to know something about the way auctions are conducted. However, it is even more important to know the property that you are bidding on and what its maximum value is to you. It is also important to exercise some self-control so that you do not get carried away in the pursuit of a popular parcel.

But that doesn't mean you should avoid auctions. Indeed, some of the best bargains have been obtained at auctions, and by people with very little experience in buying real estate.

Auctions have long carried the stigma of property dumping. The general feeling is that if you can't sell a property through normal channels, you put it up for auction. Maybe this is a carry-over from the special auction used at foreclosure sales. However, public auctions are different. The method is commonly used for such commodities as artworks and agricultural products, and these sales techniques often produce spectacular sale prices.

Generally, holders of real property resort to auctions because they think that the property will not increase in value over time and that waiting for a normal sale is not worth the carrying costs.

To that extent, the properties offered may be had for bargain prices. However, knowledgeable sellers know that an auction may produce the highest price possible for a property. They are hoping that there will be enough bidding activity from motivated buyers to result in a sale at maximum value.

Some auctions offer excellent financing to the highest bidder, regardless of his or her credit rating. Those with blemishes on their credit rating may pay above-market prices to get financed with a small down payment. In reality, when a large number of properties are sold at auction, many do go for prices above their market value. At the same time, several will sell for truly bargain prices. It depends on how much competition there is for each property.

For many properties, there is no way to tell how much they are worth. Their original sales price, in the case of previously owned properties, is no guide in a depressed market. You can make a determination, but it requires doing some homework: inspecting the property and checking with current sales of comparable properties. If you are willing to do this background checking, you will be prepared to bid intelligently for the properties you want.

Other Keys in this section will help you prepare. You will find information on how to find auction opportunities, how auctions work, how to prepare, and what you may end up with if you bid.

46

FINDING NON-FORECLOSURE AUCTION OPPORTUNITIES

From a real estate marketing standpoint, auctions are major events. Unless foreclosures are especially heavy, auctions are not conducted frequently. Therefore, you will need to keep apprised of upcoming auctions and be prepared to act when they take place.

Auction companies know that attracting a sizable crowd is the key to generating high sales prices. Consequently, a lot of effort goes into promoting the event. Look for ads in the real estate section of the local newspaper. Call auction companies or institutions that hold REO (often the auctioneers are not local, especially if the area is not a large city). If an auction is planned, they may be able to provide you with a brochure or direct you to a Web site; many auction companies have Web sites with lists or photos of properties to be sold. These properties should be open for inspection before the sale.

In areas where a lot of inventory is sold by auction, special publications have developed to inform buyers of opportunities. These publications list properties that are for sale by owners who have acquired the property through foreclosure. You can subscribe to these services or purchase individual copies of the publications.

You may prefer to operate through a real estate broker. Often, brokers can earn commissions if someone they register at an auction buys a property. Advise your broker of your interest in property auctions and let him or her keep you informed of upcoming opportunities. The broker will probably make it easier to inspect properties before the sale.

A growing avenue for publicizing events is the Internet. A keyword search will reveal a host of auction companies operating throughout the country.

47

HOW A NON-FORECLOSURE AUCTION WORKS

Once you decide to participate in a non-foreclosure auction, you should understand how these auctions are conducted. There are different types of auctions. They vary in the way bids are placed, in the way a winning bid is awarded, and in the scope of what is offered at auction. Almost all real estate auctions begin with a minimum bid suggested by the auctioneer. Bids from the audience are taken until no one is willing to outbid the last, highest bid. After a brief period, the property is awarded to the highest bidder. If no one is willing to bid the minimum price, the property may be reentered at a lower starting point or may go unsold. When a large number of properties are offered at auction, the entire bidding process for each property may last only a few minutes.

An important consideration is whether any reservations are placed on the bidding process. An absolute auction awards the property to the highest bidder no matter what the winning bid is. In this way, the seller is assured that the property will be sold (unless there are no bids at all), and the bidders are assured of getting the property at the winning bid price.

Some sellers are uncomfortable with the idea of selling at any price and may insist on a minimum bid. In this case, if no one places a bid at least as high as the minimum, the property will not be sold. This may happen when a seller is unsure of the market and is willing to hold the property if it does not bring a specified price. It may also be evidence that the seller does not completely trust the auction process, particularly when the turnout is lower than expected. (Sometimes a minimum is enforced by the courts in foreclosure sales to protect the defaulting borrower from abuse by the lender.)

The most restricted auctions are those with unstated reservation prices (Dutch or one-sided auctions). The seller can decide after the bidding whether or not to accept the highest bid. There is some question, when this tactic is used, about whether the seller really wanted to sell or merely get a feel for the market value of the property. You may not want to participate in auctions where the highest bid can be turned down.

It is also instructive to know the scope of the auction. A stand-alone auction typically deals with only one property. This is rare, except in the case of foreclosure sales. Single-owner auctions are very common. Holders of REO or developers may conduct an auction covering all or a portion of their inventory. In general, these auctions do not employ reservations or minimum bids, and the policies for bidding on each property are uniform. A multiple-owner auction may be used when several owners join together because their holdings are not large enough to justify individual auctions. In such auctions, there is a greater possibility that reservations will be placed on some properties.

In the end, your decision to participate in an auction will hinge on the quality of the properties included and any additional considerations included. For example, the seller may have arranged for financing to be offered on properties sold.

48

TIPS FOR BIDDING AT A NON-FORECLOSURE AUCTION

The key to getting a non-foreclosure auction bargain is knowing the properties you are bidding on, having a reservation price for each property, and avoiding getting caught up in the bidding frenzy. These principles should prevent you from paying too high a price for a property you expected to be a bargain (the point of going to the auction in the first place).

Knowing the properties means actually investigating each property you are interested in. Before the sale, you can obtain a list of properties that will be sold. You should have an opportunity to visit the properties. You should expend the same effort you would if you were making an offer on the property through a negotiated sales contract. If the location and other features are desirable, you may even employ a professional inspector to check over the property. If the property is a condominium, you may want to look at the legal papers that affect what you can do within the unit and the common property. (Some condos may preclude leasing out units.)

Armed with the information you find in your investigations, you can form an opinion of the property's value. This will be the basis for your reservation price, the highest price you will bid at the auction. The opening bid, the original price, and any other value information obtained at the auction are not adequate guides to how much you should pay for the property. You must form your own idea of its value.

When the actual bidding opens, the auctioneer will usually set a starting bid. This bid is set based on information from experienced buyers but may have no relationship to the actual market value of the property. The auctioneer will try to generate bidding enthusiasm by encouraging higher bids. There may be required increments by which the current bid must be raised. In some cases, it is possible to enter written bids before the auction starts. In this way, you can bid on property without having to be present at the auction. These bids are entered by the auctioneer and are valid until someone outbids the entry. If no bids exceed the written bid, the submitter wins the property at a price one increment above the next highest bid.

When bidding is active, there is a tendency for the price to rise quickly. Unless you absolutely must have the property, you should stick to your reservation price even if it means losing out. Remember that your purpose is to get a bargain. The effect of active bidding in a good auction is what causes bid prices to be at or even higher than market value appraisals for many properties.

It is always possible that bidding will be tepid enough on some properties that an uninformed bidder can end up with a good deal. When bidding is active however, there is no substitute for adequate preparation. There are no good guidelines in the bidding process to tell you how much you should bid. You must know how much the property is worth to you. It is no disgrace (nor a waste of time) to go home empty-handed.

49

PAYING FOR YOUR NON-FORECLOSURE AUCTION BUY

Being the winning bidder for the property you want is great, but you still have to finance the purchase. At the bottom of a market cycle, some buyers are able to buy so cheaply that they can pay cash or put the purchase on their credit cards. You are not likely to find such conditions very often. When you do, it may be because the property will require a lot of additional costs or will not produce income for some time.

Financing an auction purchase may be a bit more tricky than other purchases. You may need to pre-arrange credit before the auction. Most auctions allow a certain amount of time for buyers to line up their financing, recognizing that lenders require a specific piece of property to be identified before approving a loan. However, if your application is turned down, you will probably forfeit your deposit.

You should familiarize yourself with all regulations of the auction beforehand. Many require bidders to have a cashier's check or certified check for at least $500 before allowing them to enter the bidding area. Winning bidders may need to come up with some percentage of the price shortly after the auction. Find out what is required for you to bid and how much time, if any, is provided for loan approval.

Some auction sellers offer financing as a way to attract more bidders. The loans are usually provided at favorable terms compared with the market, often with a low down payment or no credit check. This is especially the case when the properties being offered are modestly priced homes. The sellers are hoping to attract homebuyers. Seller financing makes the financing problem much less troublesome. Find out what is offered before attending. Factor any financing terms into your reservation price. You can afford to pay a higher price if financing is included at below-market rates.

50

SHOULD YOU WORK WITH AN AGENT?

Real estate markets are often hard to get a handle on. Most properties are unique in some important ways that are not immediately apparent. The attractiveness, and hence value, of specific locations may vary over time. If you are not involved in the market frequently, you cannot gather and maintain the information necessary to help you reach an informed decision.

Real estate brokers and salespeople are involved in the market frequently and can be an excellent source of information. It makes sense to use their services when they can help you find the best deal. This is especially true when the service comes at no direct cost to you. (Some may argue that you are paying for this service whether you use it or not.)

Brokers and salespeople can be very useful in finding properties. Many foreclosed or bargain homes are sold like any other home, through exclusive listing contracts and the Multiple Listing Service (see Key 51). The broker can provide access to this inventory. If the property is being sold by a government agency, a broker or a salesperson may assist you in making a bid using the proper procedure and form. A broker may even represent you or accompany you to an auction.

For most people wanting to buy real estate, especially those with a day job, the question is not whether to use a broker or a salesperson but how many to use. Brokers and salespeople are in the business on a daily basis. They talk with buyers and sellers regularly and with other brokers and salespeople in their own firm and others that they deal with. By working with brokers or salespeople, you can tap into their network of contacts and knowledge of markets and properties. In fact, if you intend to be an active trader of properties, you may want to develop a rapport with an agent knowledgeable about the part of town or properties that interest you.

When you have more than one broker or salesperson helping you look, the first agent who shows you the property that you end up buying will earn a commission (some states use a procuring clause: the agent that writes the offer earns the commission). Some agents will want a buyer to work with them exclusively and will explain that they won't expend a great deal of effort if the buyer is also working with another agent. However, if the buyer is interested in more than one property and/or thinks that the broker isn't providing enough service to deserve an exclusive, the buyer should feel free to go elsewhere.

Since the early 1990s, there has been a growing movement to provide to buyers and sellers a statement disclosing just whom the broker represents. This "agency disclosure" has spawned a trend whereby brokers (or salespeople) represent buyers, trying to get a buyer the very best possible deal. This includes not only the price but also the terms of the sale, including closing date, repairs, personal property included in the sale, and so on. Most often, the broker, even a "buyer's broker," is paid by the seller. If a fee is taken from both parties, it must be disclosed. If you prefer to work with an agent professing to represent you, the buyer, go ahead. Recognize, however, that most agents will provide you with the same information on properties on the market and help you work up an offer, regardless of whom they legally represent.

51

BROKERS, SALESPEOPLE, REALTORS®, MULTIPLE LISTINGS

Most laymen are not familiar with the precise terminology of the real estate brokerage business. All fifty states in the United States have licensing requirements for the real estate industry. They license brokers, salespeople, and appraisers.

In most states, the entry level is a *salesperson* or *salesman*. To become one, a candidate must meet the state's requirements, which vary from state to state. Requirements generally include education in real estate (generally at least a 30-hour course) and passing a 2- to 3-hour, 80- to 100-question multiple-choice examination. A salesperson must also be sponsored by a licensed broker.

Although broker licensing requirements vary greatly from state to state, a broker candidate generally must have had experience (usually two to three years) as an active salesperson, must take further coursework, and must pass a more rigorous examination. Brokers are responsible for the actions of salespeople they sponsor. Brokers can do certain things that salespeople cannot. In most states, a broker's license is required for someone who helps another buy, sell, list, or lease real estate. The salesperson works as an agent for the broker; the broker is an agent of the buyer or seller.

In many situations, a broker will sponsor several salespeople. The broker may provide office space, telephone facilities, training sessions, and so on, for the sponsored salespeople. Commission splits between the broker and salesperson often depend on the volume of business generated by the salesperson and the level of service provided by the broker.

Approximately one of three real estate brokers and sales-people are members of the National Association of Realtors® (NAR). These people pay dues to NAR and also to the state and local associations of Realtors®. A licensed broker or salesperson who is also a member of NAR may prefer to be called a Realtor®, which is a registered trademark of NAR. A real estate broker or salesperson who is not a member of NAR may not be called a Realtor®.

Important to buyers and sellers in many cities is the presence of a multiple listing service (MLS). Often these are organized and run by the local board of Realtors®. Members of the MLS are required to enter all their listings into the MLS system within a short period of time—typically forty-eight to seventy-two hours. For a buyer or seller, the MLS instantly exposes the property to most of the active participants in the market. With the aid of an MLS member, a potential buyer or seller is exposed to this great information and data network.

52

SALES CONTRACTS

In most Northeastern states a *binder* is used to make an initial offer. When the offer is accepted, the owner agrees to take the property off the market and have an attorney prepare, in the next few days, a contract for the sale of the property.

In other parts of the country, a *sales contract* formalizes the negotiation process between you and the seller. This form is called a *contract of sale, agreement of sale,* or *earnest money* contract in different parts of the United States.

To make a binding offer, you must use a written contract. Contracts for the sale of real estate must be in writing to be enforceable. Besides, the seller can't respond in any meaningful way to an oral offer because there are so many details to be arranged. If you are working through a broker or agent, he or she will have preprinted standard contract forms. In some states the exact wording of the form is determined by the state agency that regulates professional real estate licenses, called the real estate commission. As an alternative, you could have an attorney draft a contract for you. However, the standard forms cover the most common items needed for the sale of a house.

You should realize that once you submit an offer in the form of a sales contract, the seller may accept your offer by signing the contract. The contract then becomes binding on both you and the seller. If the seller counteroffers, it will most likely be in the form of modifications to the contract you submitted. A counteroffer is legally a rejection of the offer and a substitution of a new offer. The counteroffer becomes binding when you initial all changes made. Negotiations become more difficult if you begin to add new requirements to the contract. Therefore, when you make your first offer, you should be careful to include all items you want in the contract.

If you have never seen a sales contract, this discussion may be a little confusing. The contract states the price you are willing to pay for the home, but it also covers all conditions attached to the sale. Remember that the price is only one point in the negotiation of a sale. Agreement must be reached on how the price is met, timing of the sale, what is included in the sale, who pays selling and financing costs, the move-in dates, and under what conditions either party can back out of the sale.

All contracts identify the seller and buyer, the property involved, and the offered price. References to the property should include a legal description and identify what is to be included (any furnishings? mineral rights?). Price should be elaborated by stating the amount of cash down payment, money to be provided through a mortgage loan, and any money paid immediately as a deposit (earnest money).

The reason financing provisions are important is that most contracts include a contingency provision in case you are turned down for the loan. If you can't get the loan, this clause allows you to recover your earnest money. At the same time, it frees the seller to offer the home to another buyer. Generally, there are separate forms for conventional, FHA, and VA financing. The seller needs to know the type of financing, since some loans require the seller to pay discount points. The type of financing used may affect the price and other points of negotiation.

Other contingencies may be placed in the contract for the protection of the buyer. You probably want to condition the sale on the property successfully passing inspections for physical condition and absence of wood-destroying insects, especially termites. These provisions give you the right to have the property inspected (at your expense). If anything is found wrong, the seller has the option of repairing the problem or, if too costly, releasing you from the contract. You may also require the right to void the sale if the property is found to be in a flood-prone (hazard) area. If you own a home currently, you may make the sale contingent on selling your home. The seller may have the right to accept backup contracts from other potential buyers. If the seller finds another buyer while the property is under contract to you subject to a contingency, you may be allowed forty-eight hours to delete the contingency and agree to close in coming days, or the seller will have the right to sell to the other party.

The contract sets a date for the closing and identifies who is responsible for the various expenses of sale. The latter provision is important if these expenses are not handled in the customary way. For example, if you want the seller to pay for discount points or if you are offering to pay the broker's commission, it should be stated in the contract. What is written in a contract is what matters. Oral promises vanish into thin air. If you do not understand a provision in the contract at any point in the negotiation, ask your broker or attorney to explain it. Make sure the explanation fits. Many brokers will not admit that they do not understand a provision in a preprinted contract. Once signed, the contract will dictate how the sale is conducted and determine how much you pay and what you will get. No changes are allowed in the contract unless the other party agrees to them.

53

NEGOTIATION

One of the keys to buying real estate is good negotiation. In the United States most prices are set by the seller, but this is not the case for real estate. Consequently, participants in a real estate transaction are often unfamiliar and uncomfortable with the bargaining process. Of course, you could accept the other party's offer and complete the transaction quickly, but that would be to your financial detriment and regret.

When negotiating a price, both seller and buyer should have an idea of their *reservation prices*. This is the minimum price the seller will accept or the maximum price the buyer can pay. If you are the seller, your reservation price may be *market value*. You figure you can get this price on the market if the deal falls through. If you are the buyer, your reservation price will be *investment value*. This is how much the property is worth to you, considering your personal situation.

The seller will add a margin to his or her reservation price, and the buyer will subtract a margin to start the bargaining. This gives each party some bargaining room. Each hopes to get a better deal than the reservation price, if possible. Whether the seller or buyer has to come close to the reservation price depends on competition in the market. If there are lots of properties on the market, the buyer is in a good position and may extract concessions from the seller. If there are lots of buyers and few good properties, the seller can insist on the reservation price. You should be aware of the competitive condition of the market when negotiating.

Bargaining starts when the buyer makes an offer for the property. The seller may accept or reject this offer, but usually comes back with a counteroffer at a higher price. The buyer then responds with another offer. The process continues until either both parties agree to terms or negotiations stop because of an impasse. Often in this process of offer and counteroffer, terms of sale other than price come into play. Either party may give in on price in return for concessions on other terms. In the process, you should keep in mind your reservation price (in terms of total costs) and try to move the negotiations toward the form of deal that best fits your situation.

Virtually everything in a property transaction is negotiable. This means not only the price but other terms such as the following:

- The form of payment (all cash at closing, deferred payments, other property)
- Who pays closing costs (the seller may pay the buyer's loan discount points, title policy premium, or other costs; the buyer may pay the seller's brokerage commission)
- Terms of financing, if the seller provides the loan (amount, interest rate, term of loan)
- Guarantees (the seller may guarantee a minimum rental income)
- Timing of closing (the buyer may wish to delay the closing to allow time to arrange financing or sign up tenants)
- Contingencies (sale subject to financing or sale of another property)

It is important to recognize that the total cost of the transaction is what counts, not merely the stated price. If you are willing to meet the seller's price, you may be able to get concessions on other items that may be more important. For example, the seller may be willing to finance the sale by lending a substantial amount of the cost. The interest rate and repayment terms then become crucial issues. Getting a lower interest rate on a long-term loan, even if only 1 percentage point lower, can be equivalent to a property price reduction of up to 10 percent.

When negotiating, you shouldn't feel that you are trying to take advantage of the other party. Recognize that offers contain margins for bargaining and that your objective is to get the best deal possible. At the same time, you must be realistic in your demands and be willing to compromise if you really want to close the deal.

54

SELLER FINANCING AND PRICE

Sometimes a piece of real estate is offered with financing. In many cases, the terms are better than those possible from outside lenders, so this type of financing can be very advantageous. Not only does it make financing the purchase easier, but the terms offer considerable savings. Indeed, the financing may make the purchase a bargain even if you pay market value for the property.

Therefore, you should take the provision of favorable financing terms into consideration when determining your reservation price. Although terms on a loan and a lump-sum price appear to be two different things, there are techniques for converting one to the other for comparison. In finance jargon, this is called *cash equivalence*, and it is a valuable tool for finding the real price paid for a property.

In essence, when you buy a property with seller financing, you are buying two items: real property and financing terms. If the terms of the loan are the same as those on other loans in the market, the terms have no special value. What makes them valuable are the monthly savings you may enjoy during the financing period. These savings are the difference between what you would have paid with market financing and what you are actually paying as a result of the seller financing. You can convert these monthly savings into a lump-sum value estimate of the savings today, called *a present value*. Doing so requires a technique called *discounting*, which simply means that a dollar in savings today is more valuable than a dollar in savings later because of potential interest earnings. Consider it a discount on the price of the property. You can base the discount on the full loan term or a shorter period if you anticipate a sale or refinancing before the loan is fully paid off.

146

An accurate estimate of cash equivalence involves some rather detailed calculations that require a financial calculator or set of tables. However, in most cases, you will not need to be highly precise in your analysis. A general idea of the magnitude of savings possible is enough to reflect it in your reservation price. The table below has been worked out as an aid in the process.

The table is based on a market rate of interest of 10 percent. If the actual rate is more or less, it will not make a big difference. The numbers in the table are the approximate percentage of discount from the asking price represented by the financing terms. In other words, you can afford to add that much more to the asking price in exchange for the financing terms. The rows refer to the percentage of the price that can be financed. The columns refer to how many percentage points the interest rate is below the market rate. Each column is divided into loans of twenty-five and twenty years.

For example, say a home is offered for $100,000. The seller will provide a loan of $75,000 (75 percent of the price) for 20 years at an interest rate one percentage point below the market. Looking at the 75 percent row and the column under one percentage point and twenty years, we find the discount to be 6 percent. A price of $106,000 (or 6 percent higher) with the financing terms is equivalent to paying $100,000 and financing with a market-rate loan.

The body of the table shows the increase in price to compensate for a below-market interest rate.

Savings (%) with Below-Market Interest Rates

| | Percentage Points Below Market Interest Rate | | | | | |
| | One Percentage Point | | Two Percentage Points | | Three Percentage Points | |
Loan/Price	25 years	20 years	25 years	20 years	25 years	20 years
100%	9	8	21	17	34	28
75%	7	6	15	13	25	21
50%	5	4	10	9	17	14

55

CONDOMINIUM CONSIDERATIONS

A large part of the foreclosure market is in condominiums. There are hundreds of thousands of "condo slaves," people who bought condos at high prices and high interest rates who can't afford to absorb a loss from a sale and don't have the cash to refinance them. For example, a person may have bought a condo for $100,000 with a $90,000 loan at 15 percent. The property is now worth $60,000, and interest rates in the market are 7 percent. However, a new lender will lend only 80 percent of current value ($48,000), which means that the present owner must present $32,000 in cash to reduce the current loan to $48,000 before it can be refinanced at 7 percent or sold at market value. This may be impossible, so the present owner continues the existing terms, absorbing the loss in high payments as a preference to abandonment with a loss in credit rating.

There are opportunities to buy condos at distressed prices. Look carefully at the situation before buying, especially at resale opportunities. All real estate, especially condos, can be like a mousetrap—easy to get into, hard to get out of. There are also some lifestyle considerations.

The biggest difference between living in a single-family detached home and a condo or co-op is the close proximity of your neighbors. When you live in a detached home, you have a buffer of lawn and maybe a fence between you and your neighbor. In a condo or co-op, this division is often no more than a common wall. In addition, once you are outside your unit, you are sharing space with the other residents. One of the most important considerations in buying a condo or co-op is deciding whether this type of living arrangement is suitable for you and your family.

Condo/co-op living does have certain advantages. Among them are these:

Cost. Multifamily housing uses less land and is often more economical to build because of common structural components and other design features. Therefore, these units are generally less expensive than detached homes of similar size and quality. (Of course, condo/co-ops can be very expensive housing when placed in exclusive locations, such as Park Avenue in New York.) Lower-priced units are good starter homes for first-time home-buyers. Lower prices mean smaller loan amounts, making it easier for young families to qualify for a mortgage. Attached units may be less expensive to heat and cool because of the insulating effect of neighboring units.

Location. Because they take less land per unit, condo/co-ops can be developed on high-cost land within major cities. This appeals to people who like being closer to downtown business and entertainment centers. On the other hand, these locations may not be as residential in character as single-family neighbor-hoods. This is a judgment you must make based on your desired lifestyle.

Low maintenance. A big attraction for some condo/co-op residents is the freedom from many of the routine household tasks. Things like lawn maintenance and outside repairs are generally the responsibility of the association or board. You pay for these services through your monthly fee, but this is often cheaper than contracting independently for these services.

Lifestyle. Some complexes are specifically designed to promote certain lifestyles. There may be organized social func-tions for young single adults. Older single people may like the security of having neighbors close by. Elaborate common area facilities may be conducive to entertaining. However, most complexes are not amenable to residents with small children or pets or those who like gardening.

There are also disadvantages to living in attached housing. This is why some people would not be happy living in a condo or co-op. If the following concerns bother you, you should consider an alternative to buying a condo/co-op.

Privacy. This is probably the biggest objection many people have to condos and co-ops. Good design can minimize this problem. Soundproofing in common walls and ceilings, private

149

entryways (often associated with townhouse designs), and private patios and decks can reduce the intrusion of your neighbors. However, attached housing frequently involves some loss of freedom.

Control. Much of what you do in your home is determined by the bylaws of the condo/co-op and majority rule of the owners association or corporation. If you cherish the independence that homeownership entails, you may not want to own a condo or co-op.

Status. In many parts of the United States, condos and co-ops are indistinguishable from rental apartments. Therefore, you may find that much of the status advantage normally attached to home-ownership is lost when you own a condo or co-op. In some areas, mortgage financing for these units has been a problem. Lenders either are unfamiliar with condo/co-op ownership or think that the units are not as marketable as, and therefore less valuable collateral than, detached homes. By contrast, a Manhattan condo or cooperative is fashionable.

Appreciation. Markets for condos have been less stable than those for detached homes. In some areas, builders have badly overestimated the market, and a surplus of condos exist. Then, too, if demand for condos increases, rental apartments can be converted quickly to increase the supply. This means your unit may not increase in value as rapidly as other types of housing.

Resale restrictions. For co-ops, the authority of the board to screen prospective tenants may complicate your ability to sell your unit for the best price. By contrast, condo sales may generally be effected without neighbors' approval.

(For more information, see Barron's *Keys to Purchasing a Condo or a Co-op.*)

56

INVESTMENT ANALYSIS

Investment analysis is deciding whether a particular investment opportunity is right for you. This involves knowing what you want and being able to figure out which investment is likely to satisfy your goals. This requires several steps. First, you must determine your investment objectives and translate them into criteria. These criteria allow you to reject inappropriate investments and pick the best of those that are appropriate. Next, decide on the type of investment: real estate, stocks, bonds, precious metals, etc. This choice depends on current asset prices and how you expect them to change in the future. It also depends on how your present investment portfolio is composed and how much diversification you need.

After you have some idea of what you want, the next step is to screen the available opportunities to eliminate those that don't fit your criteria. You may seek an expert to help you decide what to consider. When you have a set of investment alternatives that generally fit your requirements, try to decide on the best one. This consists of projecting how the investment is likely to perform, considering the chance that something will go wrong, and comparing the projected return with those offered by other investment opportunities.

There are several ways to approach investment analysis for real estate. Some investors like to review all information. Others prefer to play a hunch about what will work. Some like detailed projections. Others base their decision on inspection of the property and surrounding area. Some try to find properties that are undervalued in the market. Others emphasize negotiation to make a profitable deal. Many investors take a short-term perspective and look only at current performance. Others take a long-term viewpoint and look for value appreciation.

Regardless of the approach, you need a projection of investment return to make a decision. Since the return from real estate investments depends on future rent, operating expenses, financing, and tax considerations, by estimating these you can estimate how the property will perform. Projections may be the focus of the decision or may supplement other sources of information. The important thing to remember is that projections are only as good as the assumptions used to make them. Assuming rapid increases in rental rates and unrealistic appreciation rates can make any investment look good. It is best to take a conservative approach to the projection and let speculation about possible improved performance be a separate factor in the decision.

Short-term analysis can be used to screen properties. The following indicators may be calculated quickly with a few bits of information that are based on current performance:

Gross rent multiplier. This is the total gross rent divided by the price of the property. The lower the number, the less you are paying for the gross income. For example, a property that sells for $100,000 and rents for $1,000 per month has a multiplier of 100. If all other things were equal (operating costs, future value expectations), that would be a bargain compared with a property that costs 125 times the monthly rent.

Overall rate of return or capitalization rate. This is the net operating income (rent less operating expenses) divided by the value of the property. This measure is preferred to the gross rent multiplier because it accounts for operating expenses. Also, it offers a percentage rate, which is a customary way to express rate of return. For example, if a property rents for $1,000 per month and the owner is responsible for taxes and insurance that total $250 per month, the amount left is $750 per month. For twelve months that is $9,000, or a 9 percent return on a $100,000 investment, the overall rate of return. You should also provide a vacancy and collection allowance and detail all operating costs that the owner will bear. This example was kept simple by just indicating some likely expenses.

Cash-on-cash return or equity dividend rate. This is the cash flow divided by the required equity investment, and is especially useful when you know how the property will be financed. You may use before-tax or after-tax cash flow. If after-tax cash flow is used, you should adjust the returns on alternative types of investment for taxes to make a meaningful comparison.

Long-term analysis requires more information and assumptions because you are projecting several years into the future. If you are considering a property whose value is likely to increase or decrease in the near future, of if inflation is significant, long-term analysis is probably worthwhile.

Potential investors need to be reminded that most real estate is not a passive investment. Typically, the owner must manage the property or go to the effort of finding a property manager and giving instructions regarding management policies. The owner must then keep the manager accountable for property management, including investment results. Details of investment criteria and further explanation of real estate investment considerations are offered in Barron's *Keys to Investing in Real Estate*.

57

MARKETING YO[...]
PROPERTY FOR R[...]

Whether you have invested in a foreclosed or [...]
for immediate resale, for rental income, or to d[...]
you are likely to resell the property at some point [...]
the time horizon, you should always consider th [...]
your purchase for resale at a later date. The styl [...]
present or future curb appeal, the number of r[...]
of usable square footage, the potential for [...]
ments, the characteristics of the neighborhood [...]
high or low property taxes, the reputation of [...]
crime statistics—there is much to consider. If y[...]
weighed these and other resale attributes b[...]
should be well positioned to market the prop[...]
comes. If you have bought well below ma[...]
managed your expenses well, you may be a[...]
attractive pricing while still meeting your pr[...]
may enjoy more of a margin than anticipat[...]
able to move inventory more quickly becaus[...]
offer pricing flexibility.

Most sellers list their property with real est[...]
knowledgeable agent or broker can save [...]
pricing recommendations based on qu[...]
marketing distribution doors, identify and [...]
through fellow agents, conduct showings an[...]
marshal buyers through the generally accept[...]
avoiding the legal land mines that may acc[...]
If you are uncomfortable working directly wit[...]
and closing deals, uncertain about advert[...]
work, family, or other obligations, or nervo[...]
of bringing an agreement of sale to the p[...]
accepted by a lender, lawyer, or title co[...]

professional can offer the necessary knowledge, tools, and experience. Selling your property with a licensed professional comes at a cost, usually a percentage of the selling price. Sometimes creative fees and advertising funding can be structured. Sometimes fees can be negotiated. Sellers have to bear in mind that success at the fee negotiation table may not always translate into successful resale of a property. First, the agent who accepts a very low commission rate may not have enough self-respect to be the person you want for the job. A good real estate professional deserves to be able to earn a living. And don't forget that a portion of the commission to be earned supports advertising of your property. If you negotiate narrow terms, you may not get the advertising you need to attract prospective buyers. Second, you have to consider that, unless the listing agent also represents the buyer, as much as half or a portion of the commission you are paying typically goes to the co-broker or cooperating agent who procured the buyer. The vast majority of transactions involve more than one real estate agent/broker. If your commission negotiation is too successful, there may be little left for the cooperating agent, and therefore little incentive to look for a buyer as zealously as you might like. Once the commission amount is agreed upon, the commission split will be controlled by the listing agent unless he or she opens up a discussion about it, or unless you ask to have input. The smart seller will ask about the commission split, and will make sure all parties can be compensated in a way that assures they are all motivated, even if it means paying a larger overall percentage. The smart seller will list with a well-credentialed and well-referred real estate professional with whom he or she can enjoy an excellent business rapport.

In the real world most sellers list with agents and their brokers, but in the world of distressed real estate property, we see a considerable percentage of investors who like to resell property themselves. For Sale by Owner types, or FSBOs, as they are known, may have significant knowledge and a little bit of courage. Experienced FSBOs possess knowledge and confidence. Some like the process. Some have good sales and marketing skills. Some like to think they can do a better job than a real estate professional. Some can. And as far as can be told, 100 percent of FSBOs are trying to save real estate commission costs. FSBOs still incur expenses such as advertising, signs, open houses, automobile mileage, and wear and tear, not to mention the time and effort involved. The benefit here has to do with saving from 4 percent to as much as 7 percent of the ultimate selling price. The amount can be pretty substantial if you are fortunate enough to bring a buyer directly to the table yourself—that is, if your marketing has caused a buyer to come directly to you without having an agent. FSBOs often pay a cooperating commission fee to agents because they recognize that most available buyers are already linked to real estate agents. Anywhere from 1.5 to 3.5 percent might be offered. The higher the amount, the more motivation you may be buying. Beyond introducing a buyer, another benefit is that a cooperating agent will take the paper process out of your hands and guide all parties to closing. The most enterprising and ambitious of FSBOs will make an effort to sell the property directly for a period of fourteen to thirty days, then open up marketing to cooperating real estate professionals.

The first step for an FSBO is to establish a selling price that makes sense in the market and that can eventually be supported by an appraisal that will likely be required by a lender. Some sellers invite real estate professionals through the property to make pricing recommendations based on recent comparable home sales. If you do this with no intent to employ a listing agent or broker, it is not a very fair request of their time. If, on the other hand, you pay a real estate agent or even a certified real estate appraiser, the same professional who might conduct lender-ordered appraisals, specifically for a value or price recommendation, then you are playing the game entirely within reason. If you are in the do-it-yourself mode and think you do not want to pay or that you can develop your own comps, there are two important publicly available information sources. The tax assessor's office should be able to provide a compilation of recently sold homes in the city or town where your property is located. You may find recent sales on the very same street. You will almost certainly find homes of comparable architectural style, comparable number of rooms, bedrooms and baths, comparable square footage, comparable age, and/or comparable acreage. The most comparable homes in the most comparable locations will help you determine a fair market value. Trying to remove all emotion from the equation, you should adjust the price you establish by your eagerness to sell. The more competitively you price the property, generally the faster the sale. Test-marketing a higher price during high-demand periods can be rewarding; during lower demand, it can be risky and result in stale inventory. Another method of establishing a price is to look at properties recently sold in the tax assessor's office and compare the selling price with the property's assessed value. You may find a consistent ratio. The more homes you use in your comparable sampling, the more valid the value you establish. This is a good way to double-check looking solely at selling prices for the homes you think make the most sense. It reduces human error or misjudgment. It accepts the likely consistency and methodology used by the tax assessor. Once you have established the price at which you would like to market the property, it is time to inform interested buyers—no small task! Strategies include signage, advertising, open houses, and direct mail. Investing in a "For Sale by Owner" sign with your telephone number and possibly even an e-mail address is a basic necessity. A high-quality sign says you are a high-quality seller. You don't want a cardboard sign if you are going to instill confidence in the buyer. Additionally, you may want to consider signs of high quality for open houses and for directional signs on those days when an open house is warranted.

Creating attention-getting advertising and placing ads in the right vehicles become the next important strategies. Choosing the right newspaper(s) should not be difficult. Many others have already done the research for you with respect to the most effective vehicle. Determine where most of the real estate ads exist for the particular market in which your home is located. Double-check your assumptions by asking yourself what newspaper would be used by local residents looking for a new home and by out-of-towners looking to relocate. You may find that more than one newspaper may be appropriate to deliver your message. Then you will have the pleasure of weighing cost considerations. You will also have to determine whether to place a line ad among other classifieds, or if a display ad is going to be more productive. Scrutinize the newspaper of your choice to see how other real estate ads appear, and weighing costs, choose which ad style you think is going to be more effective. Prepare yourself for repetitive placements and a bigger ad budget whenever and wherever demand may be slow.

Although newspaper advertising is an obvious and common strategy, there are many quickly evolving Internet advertising options. These options range from free to low-cost to somewhat more ambitiously priced. Internet host sites come and go, and they are subject to frequent change, but they are always worthy of exploration and evaluation. Some sites simply list properties for sale by location as a newspaper might. Some offer the opportunity to include one or more pictures. A few offer varying levels of paid services. Some Internet sites will even insert your property in the local multiple listing service (MLS). Of course there is a loftier cost for MLS placement, and you will have to promote a co-broker real estate commission since the MLS is primarily a tool for real estate professionals. Using a search engine to identify real estate classifieds or free real estate classifieds is a beginning step. You may have read or heard about various host sites. At this writing, real estate is sold on Craigslist, Yahoo, eBay, and Lycos linked to Oodle.com. You might also look into edgeio.com, iiProperty.com linked to craigslist.org, OLX.com, owners.com, FSBO.com, ForSaleByOwner.com, ISoldMyHouse.com, USFreeads.com, Zillow.com, and ListByOwnerOnMls.com. Before you advertise online, it is recommended that you go to the site, check to be sure there are others advertising in your locale, and check for quality, ease of access for buyers, and ease of contacting you with a further inquiry; identify costs, if any, and be sure to read terms and conditions before you accept them. Have your listing data ready and your digital property photographs nearby.

Open houses are a good way to generate traffic through the property. Some buyers who are reluctant to commit to an appointment with a real estate agent will come to an open house because they feel less obligated to the seller or commitment to the real estate agent. An open house is also a good way to make contact directly with a buyer when avoiding commission expenses is among your objectives. Open-house signs are important, but you have to reach people beyond those who may be driving by the property. Newspaper advertising is common. Line ads in the classified section can work. Display ads may work better or worse, depending on ad design, newspaper layout, and how competitive advertising affects the vehicle. Ad placement in the dominant newspaper for the subject market is critical. You may also find online opportunities to serve notice of your open house at some of the aforementioned host Web sites. The best way to decide how you might like to conduct your interaction with visitors to your open house is to visit open houses yourself until you can determine what behavior works, what doesn't, and what you are comfortable in adopting without compromising who you are. In addition to evaluating the physical property, prospective buyers will want to feel that they can trust and do business with you. Empathy, truthfulness, and sincerity are excellent selling tools.

Direct mail can also be a marketing strategy for active FSBOs. There are two convenient targets and two means of approach. When dealing directly with prospective buyers who have appeared at open houses, telephoned with an inquiry, or arranged a private showing, try to obtain home or mailing addresses and e-mail addresses. By giving this information to you, the prospect has effectively opted in for future communications. With such information, you can take control of the selling relationship. You can send flyers, information updates, notice of price reductions or new incentives, and other selling communications. Regular mail can be cumbersome and less timely. E-mail is more conveniently produced, timelier, and more likely to be read. The second of two targeted audiences is real estate professionals. When you choose to invite agents and brokers into the marketing process, having names, addresses, and, better still, e-mail addresses will give you means by which to attract the interest of those who may already have buyers whose needs may be met by your property. Promoting your willingness to cooperate on a commission, particularly if the percentage you offer meets or exceeds local co-broker averages, has the potential to rapidly increase the number of prospects aware of your property.

If you are going to be in the business of marketing property yourself, you are going to need materials that inform and that help you to sell. You may remember from the last house you bought that real estate professionals work from listing sheets. These forms are intended to deliver at least one attention-getting photo and factual property data such as number of rooms and their dimensions, number of bathrooms, age of the house, garage spaces, property taxes, lot size, construction materials, heating and air-conditioning details, electric service, and water and sewer. These forms also provide space for marketing-oriented messages and driving directions to the property location. Creating your own knockoff of such a form is an essential tool in how you present your property to prospective buyers. Such forms should be constructed in a way that allows you to hand them out at open houses and during individual showings, mail them to interested parties, and e-mail them as attachments or in the body of your e-mail message. You will also field many questions about lot size, dimensions, frontage, and boundaries. It is in your interest to answer such inquiries with something visual. The tax assessor's office should be able to provide you with a map of the property. Although this map does not constitute an official survey, it is a great tool to address questions about the land on which the premises resides.

Depending on state law, you may also need to prepare disclosure documents, comments and statements about the property that must be conveyed to a prospective buyer before an agreement of sale can be executed. Where disclosures are required, you may not need to hand them out to all prospects, but you need to assure that they are in the hands of a buyer presenting an offer before a contractual commitment is made. Disclosures may include information about building materials and their current performance, septic systems, pest infestation, toxic chemicals on site, lead paint, radon in air and water, and so forth. Since guidelines vary from state to state, it is important that you check with a real estate attorney or a real estate professional to assure you are covering all of the required bases.

Finally, FSBOs must have an agreement-of-sale form ready upon need. If the buyer comes to you through a cooperating real estate agent, you can rely upon their use of an accepted agreement-of-sale form. If you are dealing directly with a buyer, however, you should have a replication of such a form that you know is going to be acceptable to the buyer's lender, attorney, and/or title company. There are numerous versions of contracts in libraries, online and in legal software packages, but you may have to consult with a local real estate attorney to obtain a form that meets with local acceptance. You should become well versed in contract contents and be able to comfortably coach a prospective buyer through its completion. Having a listing sheet, lot map, and contract form and being able to deliver these materials with confidence will serve to assure greater buyer confidence in what you are selling.

58

APPRAISALS

An appraisal is an expert opinion of value. An expert is someone with the competence and experience to do the type of analysis required. You can get opinions of value from sales agents, the owner, the tenant, or anyone familiar with the property. However, these opinions may not be very useful and probably won't be convincing as evidence of value. Usually, an appraisal expert has attained some type of designation through formal study and examination by a recognized body.

For example, the MAI and SRA designations are awarded by the Appraisal Institute to those who pass certain tests, prepare detailed sample reports called *demonstrations*, and complete years of appraisal experience. Other highly credible organizations that award appraisal designations include the National Society of Real Estate Appraisers, the American Society of Appraisers, the International Association of Assessing Officers, and the National Association of Independent Fee Appraisers. Designations from these associations assure that the appraiser understands the principles of appraisal and subscribes to a code of professional ethics. All states are now required to license appraisers of real property.

An opinion is a judgment supported by facts and logical analysis. The appraiser considers all available information that reflects on the value of the property. He or she follows a logical process to arrive at the opinion. The result is not merely a guess but a careful reading of the facts in the case. A good appraiser avoids interjecting personal bias into the opinion and tries to figure out how the market views the property.

Value should be qualified as well. There are different types of value. The majority of appraisals seek to find *market value*. This is what the property is worth to typical purchasers in a normal market. It is used as a standard in many applications. If you are interested in what the property is worth under your personal circumstances, an appraisal can be made for *investment value*. An appraiser should be able to give an opinion of value under any conditions, as long as they are spelled out at the outset.

Most appraisals are used for factual support. Lenders use them to show that a property is worth enough to serve as collateral for a loan. Appraisals may be used in condemnation cases to award compensation. They can be used to challenge property tax assessments or to back up an income tax return. They may be used in settling an estate.

Appraisals may be used as decision tools as well. You can get an appraisal to help decide how much to offer. They may serve to assist banks when trying to manage repossessed properties or to work out a troubled project.

An appraisal does not determine the market price—it is supposed to follow or reflect what is happening in the market. However, if the property under contract has been priced above the appraised value, a lender may not provide the necessary loan. Instead, the lender may suggest that the price be renegotiated to a lower amount (or force the buyer to pay the difference in cash). In doing so, the appraisal may in fact determine the market price, contradicting its purpose as stated above.

GLOSSARY

Many of the following terms were adapted from the *Real Estate Handbook* or the *Dictionary of Real Estate Terms*, copyright Barron's Educational Series, Inc., Hauppauge, New York.

Absolute auction All properties are sold to the highest bidder; the seller has no reservation prices.

Acceleration Causing the full amount of a loan to be due upon default of certain provisions.

Acceptance Agreeing to take an offer; the acceptance of an offer constitutes a contract.

Acre Measure of land containing 43,560 square feet.

Ad valorem tax Tax based on the value of the property.

Addendum An attachment to a contract, often to describe required inspections or financing terms.

Adjustable-rate mortgage (ARM) Loan where the interest rate fluctuates according to another rate, as when the mortgage rate is adjusted annually based on the one-year Treasury bill rate, plus a 2 percent margin.

Agency Legal relationship between a principal and agent arising from a contract in which the principal engages the agent to perform certain acts on the principal's behalf.

Agent One who undertakes to transact some business or to manage some affair for another, with the authority of the latter.

Agreement of sale Written agreement between buyer and seller to transfer real estate at a future date. Includes all the conditions required for a sale.

Amortization Gradual process of reducing a debt in a systematic manner.

Appraisal An expert's opinion on the value of property arrived at with careful consideration of all available and relevant data.

Appreciation Increase in the value of property.

As is Present condition of property. The "as is" clause is likely to warn of a defect.

Assessed value Value against which a property tax is imposed. The assessed value is often lower than the market value because of state law, conservative tax district appraisals, and infrequent appraisals.

Assignment Method by which a right or contract is transferred from one person to another.

Assumable mortgage Loan that can be transferred to another party. The transferee assumes the debt, but the original borrower is not released from the debt without a novation.

Auction An announced event whereby property is sold to the highest bidder. See *Absolute auction, Dutch auction.*

Balloon mortgage Loan having a large final payment.

Balloon payment Large final payment on a debt.

Bid The amount one offers to pay for real estate.

Bill of sale Document used to transfer personal property. Often used in conjunction with a real estate transaction where appliances or furniture are sold also.

Binder Brief agreement, accompanied by a deposit, showing intent to follow with a formal contract.

Bridge loan Mortgage financing between the termination of one loan and the beginning of another.

Broker One who is licensed by a state to act for property owners in real estate transactions, within the scope of state law.

Building codes Regulations established by local governments describing the minimum structural requirements for buildings; includes foundation, roofing, plumbing, electrical, and other specifications for safety and sanitation.

Cap Maximum rate of change of the interest rate on an adjustable-rate mortgage. The mortgage may have an annual or lifetime ceiling.

Capital gain Gain on the sale of a capital asset. If long-term (generally over one year), capital gains are favorably taxed.

Caveat emptor "Let the buyer beware." An expression once used in real estate to put the burden of an undisclosed defect on the buyer. This concept has been eroded in most states.

Chattels Personal property.

Clear title Title that connotes ownership free from clouds; marketable title.

Closing Date when buyer and seller exchange money for property.

Closing costs Various fees and expenses payable by the seller and buyer at the time of a real estate closing (also termed *Transaction costs*). Included are brokerage commissions, discount points, title insurance and examination, deed recording fees, and appraisal fees.

Closing statement Accounting of funds from a real estate sale, made to both the seller and the buyer separately. Most states require the broker to furnish accurate closing statements to all parties to the transaction.

Cloud on title Outstanding claim or encumbrance that, if valid, would affect or impair the owner's title. Compare *Clear title*.

Commission 1. Amount earned by a real estate broker for his services. 2. Official state agency that enforces real estate licensing laws.

Commitment letter Written pledge or promise; a firm agreement, often used to describe the terms of a mortgage loan that is being offered.

Common elements In a condominium, those portions of the property not owned individually by unit owners but in which an indivisible interest is held by all unit owners. Generally includes the grounds, parking areas, maintenance areas, recreational facilities, and external structure of the building.

Community property Property accumulated through joint efforts of husband and wife and owned by them in equal shares. This doctrine of ownership now exists in Arizona, California, Idaho, Louisiana, Nevada, New Mexico, Texas, and Washington State.

Comparables Properties that are similar to the one being sold or appraised. Used in the market approach to appraisal.

Competitive market analysis An estimate of what a property might bring based on the sale or offering of similar properties, usually by a real estate salesperson. Contrast *Appraisal*.

Conditional offer One that requires certain condition(s) to be fulfilled, such as rezoning of the property or the buyer's need to sell another property, before the contract is binding.

Conditional sales contract Written agreement for the sale of property stating that the seller retains title until the conditions of the contract have been fulfilled. See *Contract for deed*.

Condominium System of ownership of individual units in a multi-unit structure, combined with joint ownership of commonly used property (sidewalks, hallways, stairs, etc.). See *Common elements*.

Consideration Anything of value given to induce entering into a contract; it may be money, personal services, or love and affection.

Contingency Condition that must be satisfied before the party to a contract must purchase or sell. For example, financing is the most frequent contingency. A buyer who cannot arrange an appropriate loan need not complete the transaction and should receive a refund of the earnest money.

Contract Agreement between competent parties to do or not to do certain things for a consideration. Common real estate contracts are contract of sale, contract for deed, mortgage, lease, listing, deed.

Contract for deed Real estate installment sales arrangement whereby the buyer may use, occupy, and enjoy land, but no deed is given by the seller (so no title passes) until all or a specified part of the sale price has been paid. Same as *Land contract, Installment land contract, Conditional sales contract*.

Contract of sale Same as *Agreement of sale*.

Conventional loan, mortgage 1. Mortgage loan other than one guaranteed by the Department of Veterans Affairs or insured by the Federal Housing Administration. See *VA loan, FHA loan*. 2. Fixed-rate, fixed-term mortgage loan.

Cooperative Type of corporate ownership of real property whereby stockholders of the corporation are entitled to use a certain dwelling unit or other units of space. Special income tax laws allow the tenant stockholders to deduct interest and property taxes paid by the corporation.

Curtesy Right of a husband to all or part of his deceased wife's realty regardless of the provisions of her will. Exists in only a few states.

Deed Written document, properly signed and delivered, that conveys title to real property. See *General warranty deed, Quitclaim deed, Special warranty deed*.

Deed of trust Instrument used in many states in lieu of a mortgage. Legal title to the property is vested in one or more trustees to secure the repayment of the loan.

Deed restriction Clause in a deed that limits the use of land.

Default Failure to fulfill an obligation or promise or to perform specified acts.

Deficiency judgment Court order stating that the borrower still owes money when the security for a loan does not entirely satisfy a defaulted debt.

Department of Housing and Urban Development (HUD) U.S. government agency established to implement certain federal housing and community development programs.

Depreciation 1. In accounting, allocating the cost of an asset over its estimated useful life. 2. In appraisal, a charge against the reproduction cost (new) of an asset for the estimated wear and obsolescence. Depreciation may be physical, functional, or economic.

Discount points Amounts paid to the lender (often by the seller) at the time of origination of a loan, to account for the difference between the market interest rate and the lower face rate of the note.

Dower Under common law, the legal right of a wife or child to part of a deceased husband or father's property. Compare *Curtesy.*

Down payment Amount one pays for property in addition to the debt incurred.

Due-on-sale clause Provision in a mortgage that states that the loan is due upon the sale of the property.

Dutch auction The price is gradually lowered until a purchase occurs.

Earnest money Deposit made before closing by a purchaser of real estate to evidence good faith.

Easement Right, privilege, or interest that one party has in the land of another. The most common easements are for utility lines.

Encroachment Building, a part of a building, or an obstruction that physically intrudes upon, overlaps, or trespasses upon the property of another.

Encumbrance Any right to or interest in land that affects its value. Includes outstanding mortgage loans, unpaid taxes, easements, and deed restrictions.

Equity Interest or value that the owner has in real estate over and above the liens against it.

Equity loan Usually a second mortgage whereby the property owner borrows against the house, based on the value of equity built up by appreciation.

Equity of redemption The right of a borrower to regain property generally after default, before foreclosure.

Escrow Agreement between two or more parties providing that certain instruments or property be placed with a third party for safekeeping, pending the fulfillment or performance of some act or condition.

Et ux. Abbreviation of the Latin *et uxor*, which means "and wife."

Exclusive agency listing Employment contract giving only one broker, for a specified time, the right to sell the property and also allowing the owner alone to sell the property without paying a commission.

Exclusive right to sell listing Employment contract giving the broker the right to collect a commission if the property is sold by anyone, including the owner, during the term of the agreement. See *Multiple listing service*.

Execute To sign a contract; sometimes, to perform a contract fully.

Fair market value A term generally used in property tax and condemnation legislation, meaning the market value of a property.

Fannie Mae See *Federal National Mortgage Association*.

Federal Fair Housing Law Federal law that forbids discrimination on the basis of race, color, sex, religion, or national origin in the selling or renting of homes and apartments.

Federal Housing Administration (FHA) Agency within the United States Department of Housing and Urban Development that administers many loan programs, loan guarantee programs, and loan insurance programs designed to make more housing available.

Federal National Mortgage Association (FNMA) Corporation that specializes in buying mortgage loans, mostly from mortgage bankers. It adds liquidity to the mortgage market. Nicknamed Fannie Mae, FNMA is owned by its stockholders, who elect ten of its board of directors. The United States president appoints the other five directors.

Fee simple or fee absolute Absolute ownership of real property; the owner is entitled to the entire property with unconditional power of disposition during his life, and it descends to his heirs and legal representatives upon his death intestate.

FHA loan Mortgage loan insured by the FHA.

First mortgage Mortgage that has priority as a lien over all other mortgages. In cases of foreclosure, the first mortgage will be satisfied before other mortgages.

Fixed-rate mortgage Loan on which the interest rate does not change over the entire term of the loan.

Fixtures Personal property attached to the land or improvements so as to become part of the real estate.

Foreclosure Termination of all rights of a mortgagor or the grantee in the property covered by the mortgage.

For Sale by Owner See *FSBO*.

FSBO For sale by owner. A term referring to properties on the market that are not listed with a real estate broker. Also used in this book to refer to the owner-sellers. Pronounced "fizzbo."

General warranty deed Deed in which the grantor agrees to protect the grantee against any other claim to title to the property and provides other promises.

Graduated-payment mortgage (GPM) Loan requiring lower payments in early years than in later years. Payments increase in steps each year until the installments are sufficient to amortize the loan.

Grantee Party to whom the title to real property is conveyed; the buyer.

Grantor Anyone who gives a deed.

Gross rent multiplier (GRM) Sales price divided by the rental rate.

Hazard insurance A form of insurance that protects against certain risks, such as fires and storms.

Homeowners' association Organization of the homeowners in a particular subdivision, planned unit development, or condominium; generally for the purpose of enforcing deed restrictions or managing the common elements of the development.

Homeowner's policy Insurance policy designed especially for homeowners. Usually protects the owner from losses caused by most common disasters, theft, and liability. Coverage and costs vary widely.

HUD Department of Housing and Urban Development.

HUD home One that was foreclosed and offered for sale by HUD.

HUD statement Also called HUD-1 Form; see *Uniform Settlement Statement.*

Inside lot In a subdivision, a lot surrounded on each side by other lots, as opposed to a corner lot, which has road frontage on at least two sides.

Joint tenancy Ownership of real estate by two or more persons, each of whom has an undivided interest with the right of survivorship.

Junior mortgage Loan whose claim against the property will be satisfied only after prior mortgages have been repaid. See *First mortgage.*

Land contract Same as *Contract for deed.*

Lien Charge against property making it security for the payment of a debt, judgment, mortgage, or taxes; it is a type of encumbrance. A specific lien is against certain property only. A general lien is against all the property owned by the debtor.

List To give or obtain a listing.

Listing 1. Written engagement contract between a principal and an agent, authorizing the agent to perform services for the principal involving the latter's property. 2. Record of property for sale by a broker who has been authorized by the owner to sell. 3. Property so listed.

Listing agreement, listing contract Same as *Listing* (1).

Loan-to-value ratio (LTV) Amount borrowed as a percentage of the cost or value of the property purchased.

Lot and block number Method of locating a parcel of land. The description refers to a map of a subdivision that numbers each lot and block. Also called "map and lot."

Market value Most probable selling price. Also, theoretical highest price a buyer, willing but not compelled to buy, would pay, and the lowest price a seller, willing but not compelled to sell, would accept.

Mechanic's lien Lien given by law upon a building or other improvement upon land, and upon the land itself, as security for the payment for labor done and materials furnished for improvement.

Mortgage Written instrument that creates a lien upon real estate as security for the payment of a specified debt.

Mortgagee One who holds a lien on property or title to property, as security for a debt; the lender.

Mortgagor One who pledges property as security for a loan; the borrower.

Mortgage banker One who originates, sells, and services mortgage loans. Most loans are insured or guaranteed by a government agency or private mortgage insurer.

Mortgage insurance Protection for the lender in the event of default, usually covering 10 to 20 percent of the amount borrowed.

Multiple listing service (MLS) Association of real estate brokers that agrees to share listings with one another. The listing broker and the selling broker share the commission. The MLS usually distributes a book with all listings to its members, updating the book frequently. Prospective buyers benefit from the ability to select from among many homes listed by any member broker.

National Association of Real Estate Brokers (NAREB) Organization of minority real estate salespeople and brokers who are called *Realtists®*.

National Association of Realtors® (NAR) Organization of *Realtors®*, devoted to encouraging professionalism in real estate activities. There are more than 1,300,000 members of NAR, 50 state associations, and several affiliates.

Negative amortization Increase in the outstanding balance of a loan resulting from the failure of periodic debt service payments to cover required interest charged on the loan.

Net listing Listing in which the broker's commission is the excess of the sales price over an agreed-upon (net) price to the seller; illegal in some states.

Notary public Officer who is authorized to take acknowledgments to certain types of documents, such as deeds, contracts, and mortgages, and before whom affidavits may be sworn.

Novation Agreement whereby a lender substitutes one party to a contract for another, releasing the original party from any obligation.

Offer Expression of willingness to purchase a property at a specified price.

Open house Method of showing a home for sale whereby the home is open for inspection on an advertised date.

Open housing Condition under which housing units may be purchased or leased without regard for racial, ethnic, color, or religious characteristics of the buyers or tenants.

Open listing Listing given to any number of brokers without liability to compensate any except the one who first secures a buyer who is ready, willing, and able to meet the terms of the listing or secures the seller's acceptance of another offer. The sale of the property automatically terminates all open listings.

Oral contract Unwritten agreement. With few exceptions, oral agreements for the sale or use of real estate are unenforceable. In most states, contracts for the sale or rental of real estate, unless they are in writing, are unenforceable under the Statute of Frauds. Oral leases for a year or less are often acceptable.

ORE, OREO See *REO*.

Origination fees Charges to a borrower to cover the costs of issuing a loan, such as credit checks, appraisal, and title expenses. Origination fees are sometimes quoted as a percentage of the amount borrowed, in addition to specifically identified expenses.

Performance bond Assures that a contractor will perform in accordance with the contract and protects against a breach of contract.

Permanent mortgage Mortgage for a long period of time (over ten years).

Plat Plan or map of a specific land area.

Points See *Discount points*.

Pre-foreclosure sale Purchase of a home from a borrower who is in default on the mortgage loan before the lender forecloses the mortgage.

Prepayment penalty Penalty imposed on a borrower when a loan is retired before maturity.

Prepayment privilege Right of a borrower to retire a loan before maturity.

Principal 1. One who owns or will use property. 2. One who contracts for the services of an agent or broker; the broker's or agent's client. 3. The amount of money raised by a mortgage or other loan, as distinct from the interest paid on it.

Principal and interest payment (P&I) Periodic payment, usually made monthly, that includes the interest charges for the period plus an amount applied to amortization of the principal balance. Commonly used with self-amortizing loans.

Principal, interest, taxes, and insurance (PITI) Monthly mortgage payment (P&I), with the addition of an amount deposited in escrow for future payment of taxes and insurance.

Private mortgage insurance (PMI) See *Mortgage insurance*.

Property tax A government levy based on the market value of privately owned property. Sometimes referred to as *Ad valorem tax* or real estate tax.

Prorate To allocate between seller and buyer their proportionate shares of an obligation paid or due; for example, to prorate real estate taxes.

Purchase-money mortgage Mortgage given by a grantee (buyer) to a grantor (seller) in part payment of the purchase price of real estate.

Quitclaim deed Deed that conveys only the grantor's rights or interest in real estate, without stating the nature of the rights and with no warranties of ownership. Often used to remove a possible cloud on the title. Contrast with *General warranty deed*.

Real estate 1. In law, land and everything more or less attached to it. Ownership below to the center of the earth and above to the heavens. Distinguished from *personal property*. Same as *realty*. 2. In business, the activities concerned with ownership and use transfers of the physical property.

Real estate agent A licensed real estate broker or salesperson; see *Agent*. Often refers to a licensed salesperson, who must work under a licensed broker.

Real estate broker A state-licensed *Agent* who, for a fee, acts for property owners in real estate transactions, within the scope of state law. A broker's license typically requires a higher level of education, experience as real estate salesperson, and passing another examination. Brokers are typically permitted to open their own agencies, whereas real estate salespersons may not.

Real Estate Settlement Procedures Act (RESPA) Law that states how mortgage lenders must treat those who apply for federally related real estate loans on property with one to four dwelling units. Intended to provide borrowers with more knowledge when they comparison shop for mortgage money.

Realtist® Member of the National Association of Real Estate Brokers, a group composed primarily of minority brokers.

Realtor® A professional in real estate who subscribes to a strict code of ethics as a member of the local and state boards and of the National Association of Realtors®.

Redlining Illegal practice of refusing to originate mortgage loans in certain neighborhoods on the basis of race or ethnic composition.

Refinance To substitute a new loan for an old one, often in order to borrow more or to reduce the interest rate.

REO Real estate owned; also, other real estate (ORE). Refers to real estate owned by banks that is not used for banking operations.

Repossession Commonly used to mean the same as foreclosure; property claimed by lender for violation of a loan provision, usually nonpayment.

Reservation price A mental note of the minimum a seller will accept; the maximum a buyer will pay.

Sales contract Same as *Contract of sale*.

Sealed bids Offers submitted in a closed envelope so that other bidders do not see what others are willing to pay.

Secondary mortgage market The "marketplace" where existing mortgages, mostly first mortgages on homes, are traded.

Self-amortizing mortgage Loan that will retire itself through regular principal and interest payments. Contrast with *Balloon mortgage*.

Sellers' market Economic conditions that favor sellers, reflecting rising prices and market activity.

Settlement Same as *Closing*.

Short sale A *Pre-foreclosure sale* in which the lender agrees to take less than the outstanding balance of the mortgage loan. The defaulting borrower avoids having the default reported to the credit bureaus, the lender gets as much or more than would have been received in foreclosure, and the buyer gets a below-market price on the home.

Special assessment Assessment made against a property to pay for a public improvement by which the assessed property is supposed to be especially benefited.

Special warranty deed Deed in which the grantor limits the title warranty given to the grantee to anyone claiming by, from, through, or under him, the grantor. The grantor does not warrant against title defects arising from conditions that existed before he owned the property. Often this type of deed is quite satisfactory. For example, a buyer in a foreclosure sale will receive a sheriff's deed, which is a special warranty against claims arising before foreclosure.

Specific performance Legal action in which the court requires a party to a contract to perform the terms of the contract when he has refused to fulfill his obligations. Used in real estate, since each parcel of land is unique.

Statutory According to statutes; pertaining to written laws.

Statutory redemption The right of a borrower to regain property that was foreclosed, according to written law.

Subcontractor One who performs services under contract to a general contractor.

Subdivision Tract of land divided into lots or plots suitable for home-building purposes. Some states and localities require that a subdivision plot be recorded.

Subject to mortgage Arrangement whereby a buyer takes title to mortgaged real property but is not personally responsible for the payment of any portion of the amount due. The buyer must make payments in order to keep the property; however, if he fails to do so, only his equity in that property is lost.

Survey Process by which a parcel of land is measured and its area ascertained; also, the blueprint showing the measurements, boundaries, and area.

Sweat equity Value added to a property because of improvements as a result of work performed personally by the owner.

Term amortization For a loan, the period of time during which principal and interest payments must be made; generally, the time needed to amortize the loan fully.

Terms Provisions in a contract; interest rate and payment requirements of a loan.

Title Evidence that the owner of land is in lawful possession thereof; evidence of ownership.

Title insurance Insurance policy that protects the holder from loss sustained by defects in the title.

Title search Examination of the public records to determine the ownership and encumbrances affecting real property.

Transfer tax Tax paid on the passing of *Title* to property or to a valuable interest. Sometimes called *transfer stamps*.

Veterans Affairs (VA) Government department that guarantees home mortgage loans to discharged service members.

VA loan (mortgage) Loan that is guaranteed by the Department of Veterans Affairs. Honorably discharged service members with 90 days' service in time of war or 180 days in time of peace (90 days during Desert Storm) or 6 years active service in federal or state reserves are eligible.

Vendee Buyer.

Vendor Seller.

Warranty deed Title to real estate in which the grantor guarantees title. Usually protects against other claimants, liens, or encumbrances and offers good title.

Zoning ordinance Act of city, county, or other authorities specifying the type of use to which property may be put in specific areas. Examples: residential, commercial, industrial.

CHECKLIST

A good checklist is a useful device to try to ensure that nothing has been overlooked. Although a perfect home has yet to be built, a checklist may help determine whether a house has so many negatives that it is unsuitable for you, or has a "fatal flaw"—something you wouldn't want to own at any price. Use the list to help jog your memory about each feature.

General Checklist

Address
Date shown
Shown by
Owner's name
Phone number
Reason for selling
Availability or Urgency of sale
Age
Price
Special financing
  Assumption, seller
Loan status:
  Delinquent

Default
Foreclosed by
Local institution
HUD
VA
Private mortgage insurer
Relocation company ownership
Taxes
Builder
Style, stories, or levels
Construction quality
Comments

Location Characteristics

Superior   Average   Inferior

School district
  Elementary
  Junior high
  High
  Parochial
Fire and police protection
Transportation
Medical facilities

Shopping
Recreational
Religious facilities
Neighborhood
Subdivision
Homeowner association
View
Crime statistics in neighborhood
Registry of sexual offenders living in area

Interior Arrangements

	Superior	Average	Inferior
Number of bedrooms			
Closet(s) size, shelving			
Number of bathrooms			
Size, fixtures, floor			
Living room			
Family room			
Laundry/utility room			
Floor plan			
Floor coverings			
Window treatments			
Built-in cabinets			
Paint			
Wallpaper			
Fireplace			
Basement			
Additional comments			

House Exterior—Quality or Condition

	Superior	Average	Inferior
Roof			
Façade			
Windows			
Drainage			
Paint			
Garage (size, attached)			
Attic			
Storage			
Additional comments			

Lot

	Superior	Average	Inferior

Size, shape
Fence
Shrubbery
Trees
Lawn
Sprinklers
Swimming pool
Patio
Driveway
Traffic
Zoning
Floodplain
Easements
Environmental hazards
   Asbestos
   Lead paint
   Radon (air)
   Radon (water)
Additional comments

Servicing

	Superior	Average	Inferior

Waste (sewer, septic)
Heating
Air-conditioning
Insulation
   Ceiling
   Walls
   Weather-stripping
   Storm windows, doors
Wiring, electrical capacity
Plumbing
Appliances
Additional comments

Negotiating

Asking price
Probable price
Financing

Points or origination fees
Closing costs
  Legal
  Recording
  Appraisal
Inspections
  Inside
  Outside
  Pests
  Environmental
Contingencies
  Sale of old house
  Mortgage approval
  Mortgage terms
Additional comments

Financing

Existing financing
  Assumability
  Lender(s), account numbers, phone numbers
  Unpaid balance(s), interest rate, remaining term, balloons
  Transfer fees
  Prepayment penalty
New Financing

Lender Name Phone #	Type of Loan	Interest Rate	Loan-to- Value Ratio	Loan Term (Years)	Points	Fees	Lock-in

Legal Considerations

Deed type
Homestead exemption
Spouse's name
Ownership form
  (joint tenancy, community property)
Title policy or abstract
Exceptions on title policy
Attorney's opinion of title
Additional comments

PAYMENT TABLES

To calculate monthly payment requirements from tables on following pages:

1. Find intersection of Contract Interest Rate with Term (Years).
2. Multiply amount in table by thousands borrowed to result in monthly principal and interest payment.
3. Add estimated taxes and insurance (not shown on table).

Example: Find the monthly payment on a $90,000 loan for 25 years at 9½ percent interest.

Step 1.   8.74 (read from table).

Step 2.   Multiply by 90.
          Result $786.60 is the monthly principal and interest payment.

Step 3.   Add monthly tax and insurance requirement.

Monthly Principal and Interest Payments
per $1,000 of Principal

Term (Years)	Contract Interest Rate (%)			
	5.00	5.25	5.50	5.75
1	85.61	85.72	85.84	85.95
2	43.87	43.98	44.10	44.21
3	29.97	30.08	30.20	30.31
4	23.03	23.14	23.26	23.37
5	18.87	18.99	19.10	19.22
6	16.10	16.22	16.34	16.46
7	14.13	14.25	14.37	14.49
8	12.66	12.78	12.90	13.02
9	11.52	11.64	11.76	11.88
10	10.61	10.73	10.85	10.98
11	9.86	9.99	10.11	10.24
12	9.25	9.37	9.50	9.63
13	8.73	8.86	8.99	9.12
14	8.29	8.42	8.55	8.68
15	7.91	8.04	8.17	8.30
16	7.58	7.71	7.84	7.98
17	7.29	7.42	7.56	7.69
18	7.03	7.17	7.30	7.44
19	6.80	6.94	7.08	7.22
20	6.60	6.74	6.88	7.02
21	6.42	6.56	6.70	6.84
22	6.25	6.39	6.54	6.68
23	6.10	6.25	6.39	6.54
24	5.97	6.11	6.26	6.41
25	5.85	5.99	6.14	6.29
26	5.73	5.88	6.03	6.18
27	5.63	5.78	5.93	6.08
28	5.54	5.69	5.84	5.99
29	5.45	5.60	5.76	5.91
30	5.37	5.52	5.68	5.84

Monthly Principal and Interest Payments
per $1,000 of Principal

Term (Years)	Contract Interest Rate (%) 6.00	6.25	6.50	6.75
1	86.07	86.18	86.30	86.41
2	44.32	44.43	44.55	44.66
3	30.42	30.54	30.65	30.76
4	23.49	23.60	23.71	23.83
5	19.33	19.45	19.57	19.68
6	16.57	16.69	16.81	16.93
7	14.61	14.73	14.85	14.97
8	13.14	13.26	13.39	13.51
9	12.01	12.13	12.25	12.38
10	11.10	11.23	11.35	11.48
11	10.37	10.49	10.62	10.75
12	9.76	9.89	10.02	10.15
13	9.25	9.38	9.51	9.65
14	8.81	8.95	9.08	9.22
15	8.44	8.57	8.71	8.85
16	8.11	8.25	8.39	8.53
17	7.83	7.97	8.11	8.25
18	7.58	7.72	7.87	8.01
19	7.36	7.50	7.65	7.79
20	7.16	7.31	7.46	7.60
21	6.99	7.14	7.28	7.43
22	6.83	6.98	7.13	7.28
23	6.69	6.84	6.99	7.14
24	6.56	6.71	6.87	7.02
25	6.44	6.60	6.75	6.91
26	6.34	6.49	6.65	6.81
27	6.24	6.40	6.56	6.72
28	6.15	6.31	6.47	6.63
29	6.07	6.23	6.39	6.56
30	6.00	6.16	6.32	6.49

Monthly Principal and Interest Payments
per $1,000 of Principal

Term (Years)	Contract Interest Rate (%) 7.00	7.25	7.50	7.75
1	86.53	86.64	86.76	86.87
2	44.77	44.89	45.00	45.11
3	30.88	30.99	31.11	31.22
4	23.95	24.06	24.18	24.30
5	19.80	19.92	20.04	20.16
6	17.05	17.17	17.29	17.41
7	15.09	15.22	15.34	15.46
8	13.63	13.76	13.88	14.01
9	12.51	12.63	12.76	12.89
10	11.61	11.74	11.87	12.00
11	10.88	11.02	11.15	11.28
12	10.28	10.42	10.55	10.69
13	9.78	9.92	10.05	10.19
14	9.35	9.49	9.63	9.77
15	8.99	9.13	9.27	9.41
16	8.67	8.81	8.96	9.10
17	8.40	8.54	8.69	8.83
18	8.16	8.30	8.45	8.60
19	7.94	8.09	8.24	8.39
20	7.75	7.90	8.06	8.21
21	7.58	7.74	7.89	8.05
22	7.43	7.59	7.75	7.90
23	7.30	7.46	7.61	7.77
24	7.18	7.34	7.50	7.66
25	7.07	7.23	7.39	7.55
26	6.97	7.13	7.29	7.46
27	6.88	7.04	7.21	7.37
28	6.80	6.96	7.13	7.30
29	6.72	6.89	7.06	7.23
30	6.65	6.82	6.99	7.16

Monthly Principal and Interest Payments
per $1,000 of Principal

Term (Years)	Contract Interest Rate (%) 8.00	8.25	8.50	8.75
1	86.99	87.10	87.22	87.34
2	45.23	45.34	45.46	45.57
3	31.34	31.45	31.57	31.68
4	24.41	24.53	24.65	24.77
5	20.28	20.40	20.52	20.64
6	17.53	17.66	17.78	17.90
7	15.59	15.71	15.84	15.96
8	14.14	14.26	14.39	14.52
9	13.02	13.15	13.28	13.41
10	12.13	12.27	12.40	12.53
11	11.42	11.55	11.69	11.82
12	10.82	10.96	11.10	11.24
13	10.33	10.47	10.61	10.75
14	9.91	10.06	10.20	10.34
15	9.56	9.70	9.85	9.99
16	9.25	9.40	9.54	9.69
17	8.98	9.13	9.28	9.43
18	8.75	8.90	9.05	9.21
19	8.55	8.70	8.85	9.01
20	8.36	8.52	8.68	8.84
21	8.20	8.36	8.52	8.68
22	8.06	8.22	8.38	8.55
23	7.93	8.10	8.26	8.43
24	7.82	7.98	8.15	8.32
25	7.72	7.88	8.05	8.22
26	7.63	7.79	7.96	8.13
27	7.54	7.71	7.88	8.06
28	7.47	7.64	7.81	7.99
29	7.40	7.57	7.75	7.92
30	7.34	7.51	7.69	7.87

Monthly Principal and Interest Payments
per $1,000 of Principal

Term (Years)	9.00	9.25	9.50	9.75
	Contract Interest Rate (%)			
1	87.45	87.57	87.68	87.80
2	45.68	45.80	45.91	46.03
3	31.80	31.92	32.03	32.15
4	24.88	25.00	25.12	25.24
5	20.76	20.88	21.00	21.12
6	18.03	18.15	18.27	18.40
7	16.09	16.22	16.34	16.47
8	14.65	14.78	14.91	15.04
9	13.54	13.68	13.81	13.94
10	12.67	12.80	12.94	13.08
11	11.96	12.10	12.24	12.38
12	11.38	11.52	11.66	11.81
13	10.90	11.04	11.19	11.33
14	10.49	10.64	10.78	10.93
15	10.14	10.29	10.44	10.59
16	9.85	10.00	10.15	10.30
17	9.59	9.74	9.90	10.05
18	9.36	9.52	9.68	9.84
19	9.17	9.33	9.49	9.65
20	9.00	9.16	9.32	9.49
21	8.85	9.01	9.17	9.34
22	8.71	8.88	9.04	9.21
23	8.59	8.76	8.93	9.10
24	8.49	8.66	8.83	9.00
25	8.39	8.56	8.74	8.91
26	8.31	8.48	8.66	8.83
27	8.23	8.41	8.58	8.76
28	8.16	8.34	8.52	8.70
29	8.10	8.28	8.46	8.64
30	8.05	8.23	8.41	8.59

Monthly Principal and Interest Payments
per $1,000 of Principal

Term (Years)	Contract Interest Rate (%)			
	10.00	**10.25**	**10.50**	**10.75**
1	87.92	88.03	88.15	88.27
2	46.15	46.26	46.38	46.49
3	32.27	32.38	32.50	32.62
4	25.36	25.48	25.60	25.72
5	21.25	21.37	21.49	21.62
6	18.53	18.65	18.78	18.91
7	16.60	16.73	16.86	16.99
8	15.17	15.31	15.44	15.57
9	14.08	14.21	14.35	14.49
10	13.22	13.35	13.49	13.63
11	12.52	12.66	12.80	12.95
12	11.95	12.10	12.24	12.39
13	11.48	11.63	11.78	11.92
14	11.08	11.23	11.38	11.54
15	10.75	10.90	11.05	11.21
16	10.46	10.62	10.77	10.93
17	10.21	10.37	10.53	10.69
18	10.00	10.16	10.32	10.49
19	9.81	9.98	10.14	10.31
20	9.65	9.82	9.98	10.15
21	9.51	9.68	9.85	10.02
22	9.38	9.55	9.73	9.90
23	9.27	9.44	9.62	9.79
24	9.17	9.35	9.52	9.70
25	9.09	9.26	9.44	9.62
26	9.01	9.19	9.37	9.55
27	8.94	9.12	9.30	9.49
28	8.88	9.06	9.25	9.43
29	8.82	9.01	9.19	9.38
30	8.78	8.96	9.15	9.33

Monthly Principal and Interest Payments
per $1,000 of Principal

Term (Years)	Contract Interest Rate (%) 11.00	11.25	11.50	11.75
1	88.38	88.50	88.62	88.73
2	46.61	46.72	46.84	46.96
3	32.74	32.86	32.98	33.10
4	25.85	25.97	26.09	26.21
5	21.74	21.87	21.99	22.12
6	19.03	19.16	19.29	19.42
7	17.12	17.25	17.39	17.52
8	15.71	15.84	15.98	16.12
9	14.63	14.76	14.90	15.04
10	13.77	13.92	14.06	14.20
11	13.09	13.24	13.38	13.53
12	12.54	12.68	12.83	12.98
13	12.08	12.23	12.38	12.53
14	11.69	11.85	12.00	12.16
15	11.37	11.52	11.68	11.84
16	11.09	11.25	11.41	11.57
17	10.85	11.02	11.18	11.35
18	10.65	10.82	10.98	11.15
19	10.47	10.64	10.81	10.98
20	10.32	10.49	10.66	10.84
21	10.19	10.36	10.54	10.71
22	10.07	10.25	10.42	10.60
23	9.97	10.15	10.33	10.51
24	9.88	10.06	10.24	10.42
25	9.80	9.98	10.16	10.35
26	9.73	9.91	10.10	10.28
27	9.67	9.85	10.04	10.23
28	9.61	9.80	9.99	10.18
29	9.57	9.75	9.94	10.13
30	9.52	9.71	9.90	10.09

Monthly Principal and Interest Payments
per $1,000 of Principal

Term (Years)	Contract Interest Rate (%)			
	12.00	12.25	12.50	12.75
1	88.85	88.97	89.08	89.20
2	47.07	47.19	47.31	47.42
3	33.21	33.33	33.45	33.57
4	26.33	26.46	26.58	26.70
5	22.24	22.37	22.50	22.63
6	19.55	19.68	19.81	19.94
7	17.65	17.79	17.92	18.06
8	16.25	16.39	16.53	16.67
9	15.18	15.33	15.47	15.61
10	14.35	14.49	14.64	14.78
11	13.68	13.83	13.98	14.13
12	13.13	13.29	13.44	13.59
13	12.69	12.84	13.00	13.15
14	12.31	12.47	12.63	12.79
15	12.00	12.16	12.33	12.49
16	11.74	11.90	12.07	12.23
17	11.51	11.68	11.85	12.02
18	11.32	11.49	11.66	11.83
19	11.15	11.33	11.50	11.67
20	11.01	11.19	11.36	11.54
21	10.89	11.06	11.24	11.42
22	10.78	10.96	11.14	11.32
23	10.69	10.87	11.05	11.23
24	10.60	10.79	10.97	11.16
25	10.53	10.72	10.90	11.09
26	10.47	10.66	10.84	11.03
27	10.41	10.60	10.79	10.98
28	10.37	10.56	10.75	10.94
29	10.32	10.52	10.71	10.90
30	10.29	10.48	10.67	10.87

AGENCY FIELD OFFICES

HUD

Region I (Boston)

Boston Regional Office
10 Causeway Street, Room 301
Boston, MA 02222-1092
(617) 565-5236

Bangor
202 Harlow Street, Room 101
Bangor, ME 04401-4919
(207) 945-0467

Burlington
159 Bank Street, 2nd Floor
P.O. Box 879
Burlington, VT 05402-0879
(802) 951-6290

Hartford
20 Church Street, 19th Floor
Hartford, CT 06103-3220
(860) 240-4800

Manchester
1000 Elm Street, 8th Floor
Manchester, NH 03101-1730
(603) 666-7441

Providence
121 S. Main Street, Suite 300
Providence, RI 02903-7104
(401) 528-5351

Region II (New York)

New York Regional Office
26 Federal Plaza, Room 3541
New York, NY 10278-0068
(212) 264-8000

Albany
52 Corporate Circle
Albany, NY 12203-5121
(518) 464-4200

Buffalo
Lafayette Court, 2nd Floor
465 Main Street
Buffalo, NY 14203-1780
(716) 551-5755

Camden
Hudson Building, 2nd Floor
800 Hudson Square
Camden, NJ 08102-1156
(856) 757-5081

Caribbean
235 Federico Costa Street, Suite 200
San Juan, PR 00918
(787) 766-5201

Newark
One Newark Center, 13th Floor
Newark, NJ 07102-5260
(973) 622-7900

Philadelphia Regional Office
The Wanamaker Building
100 Penn Square East
Philadelphia, PA 19107-3380
(215) 656-0500

Baltimore
10 S. Howard Street, 5th Floor
Baltimore, MD 21201-2505
(410) 962-2520

Charleston
505 Capitol Street, Suite 708
Charleston, WV 25301-1795
(304) 347-7000

Pittsburgh
339 Sixth Avenue, 6th Floor
Pittsburgh, PA 15222-2515
(412) 644-6428

Richmond
600 E. Broad Street
Richmond, VA 23219-4920
(804) 771-2100

Washington, DC
820 First Street NE, Suite 300
Washington, DC 20002-4205
(202) 275-9200

Wilmington
920 King Street, Suite 404
Wilmington, DE 19801-3016
(302) 573-6300

Region IV (Atlanta)

Atlanta Regional Office
40 Marietta Street
Five Points Plaza
Atlanta, GA 30303-2806
(404) 331-4111

Birmingham
950 22nd Street North, Suite 900
Birmingham, AL 35203-5302
(205) 731-2617

Columbia
1835 Assembly Street, 13th Floor
Columbia, SC 29201-2480
(803) 765-5592

Greensboro
Asheville Building
1500 Pinecroft Road, Suite 401
Greensboro, NC 27407-3838
(336) 547-4001

Jackson
100 W. Capitol Street, Room 910
Jackson, MS 39269-1096
(601) 965-4757

Jacksonville
400 W. Bay Street, Suite 1015
Jacksonville, FL 32202-4439
(904) 232-2627

Knoxville
710 Locust Street SW, Suite 300
Knoxville, TN 37902-2526
(865) 545-4400

Louisville
601 W. Broadway
Louisville, KY 40202
(502) 582-5251

Memphis
200 Jefferson Avenue, Suite 300
Memphis, TN 38103-2389
(901) 544-3367

Miami
909 SE First Avenue, Room 500
Miami, FL 33131-3028
(305) 536-4456

Nashville
235 Cumberland Bend Drive,
Suite 200
Nashville, TN 37228-1803
(615) 736-5213

Orlando
Langley Building, Suite 270
3751 Maguire Boulevard
Orlando, FL 32803-3032
(407) 648-6441

Tampa
500 Zack Street, Suite 402
Tampa, FL 33602-3918
(813) 228-2026

Region V (Chicago)

Chicago Regional Office
Ralph H. Metcalfe Federal
Building
77 W. Jackson Boulevard
Chicago, IL 60604-3507
(312) 353-5680

Cincinnati
15 E. Seventh Street
Cincinnati, OH 45202-2401
(513) 684-3451

Cleveland
1350 Euclid Avenue, Suite 500
Cleveland, OH 44115-1815
(216) 522-4058

Columbus
200 N. High Street
Columbus, OH 43215-2463
(614) 469-2540

Detroit
477 Michigan Avenue
Detroit, MI 48226-2592
(313) 226-7900

Flint
Phoenix Building
801 S. Saginaw Street, 4th Floor
Flint, MI 48502-1511
(810) 766-5112

Grand Rapids
Trade Center Building
50 Louis Street NW
Grand Rapids, MI 49503-2633
(616) 456-2100

Indianapolis
151 N. Delaware Street, Suite
1200
Indianapolis, IN 46204-2526
(317) 226-6303

Milwaukee
310 W. Wisconsin Avenue, Room
1380
Milwaukee, WI 53203-2289
(414) 297-3214

Minneapolis
920 Second Avenue South
Minneapolis, MN 55402
(612) 370-3000

Region VI (Fort Worth)

Fort Worth Regional Office
801 Cherry Street, Unit #45,
Suite 2500
Fort Worth, TX 76102-6882
(817) 978-5965

Albuquerque
625 Silver Avenue SW, Suite 100
Albuquerque, NM 87102-3185
(505) 346-6463

Dallas
525 S. Griffin Street, Room 860
Dallas, TX 75202-5032
(214) 767-8300

Houston
1301 Fannin Street, Suite 2200
Houston, TX 77002-7008
(713) 718-3199

Little Rock
425 W. Capitol Avenue, Suite 900
Little Rock, AR 72201-3488
(501) 324-5931

Lubbock
1205 Texas Avenue, Room 511
Lubbock, TX 79401-4093
(806) 472-7265

New Orleans
500 Poydras Street, 9th Floor
New Orleans, LA 70130-3328
(504) 589-7201

Oklahoma City
301 NW 6th Street, Suite 200
Oklahoma City, OK 73102-2811
(405) 609-8509

San Antonio
106 S. St. Mary's Street, Suite 405
San Antonio, TX 78205-3625
(210) 475-6806

Shreveport
401 Edwards Street, Room 1510
Shreveport, LA 71101-5513
(318) 676-3440

Tulsa
2 W. Second Street, Suite 400
Tulsa, OK 74103-3122
(918) 292-8900

Region VII (Kansas City)

Kansas City Regional Office
400 State Avenue, Room 200
Kansas City, KS 66101-2406
(913) 551-5462

Des Moines
210 Walnut Street, Room 239
Des Moines, IA 50309-2155
(515) 284-4512

Omaha
10909 Mill Valley Road
Omaha, NE 68154-3955
(402) 492-3101

St. Louis
1222 Spruce Street, Suite 3207
St. Louis, MO 63103-2836
(314) 539-6583

Region VIII (Denver)

Denver Regional Office
1670 Broadway, 23rd Floor
Denver, CO 80202-3606
(303) 672-5440

Casper
150 East B Street, Room 1010
Casper, WY 82601-1969
(307) 261-6250

Fargo
657 Second Avenue North, Room 366
Fargo, ND 58108-4727
(701) 239-5136

Helena
7 W. 6th Avenue
Helena, MT 59601
(406) 449-5050

Salt Lake City
151 S. State Street, Suite 3001
Salt Lake City, UT 84138
(801) 524-6070

Sioux Falls
2400 W. 49th Street, Room I-201
Sioux Falls, SD 57105-6558
(605) 330-4223

San Francisco Regional Office
600 Harrison Street, 3rd Floor
San Francisco, CA 94107-1300
(415) 489-6400

Fresno
2135 Fresno Street, Suite 100
Fresno, CA 93721-1718
(559) 487-5033

Honolulu
500 Ala Moana Boulevard, Suite 3A
Honolulu, HI 96813-4918
(808) 522-8175

Las Vegas
300 S. Las Vegas Boulevard, Suite 2900
Las Vegas, NV 89101-5833
(702) 366-2100

Los Angeles
611 W. Sixth Street, Suite 800
Los Angeles, CA 90017-3101
(213) 894-8000

Phoenix
One N. Central Avenue, Suite 600
Phoenix, AZ 85004-4415
(602) 379-7100

Reno
3702 S. Virginia Street
Reno, NV 89502-6581
(775) 784-5383

Sacramento
650 Capitol Mall, Room 4-200
Sacramento, CA 95814-4708
(916) 498-5220

San Diego
750 B Street, Suite 1600
San Diego, CA 92101-8131
(619) 557-5310

Santa Ana
34 Civic Center Plaza, Room 7015
Santa Ana, CA 92701-4003
(714) 796-5577

Tucson
160 N. Stone Avenue
Tucson, AZ 85701-1467
(520) 670-6000

Region X (Seattle)

Seattle Regional Office
909 First Avenue, Suite 200
Seattle, WA 98104-1000
(206) 220-5101

Anchorage
3000 C Street, Suite 401
Anchorage, AK 99503-3975
(907) 677-9800

Boise
800 Park Boulevard, Suite 220
Boise, ID 83712-7743
(208) 334-1990

Portland
400 SW 6th Avenue, Suite 700
Portland, OR 97204-1632
(971) 222-2600

Spokane
920 W. Riverside Avenue, Suite 588
Spokane, WA 99201-1010
(509) 368-3200

VA

(Note: Locate your closest local facility from http://www1.va.gov/directory/guide/home.asp. Unless otherwise noted, all addresses below are for VA Regional Offices.)

Alabama
345 Perry Hill Road
Montgomery, AL 36109-3798

Alaska
VA Outpatient Clinic & Regional Office
2925 Debarr Road
Anchorage, AK 99508-2989

Arizona
3333 N. Central Avenue
Phoenix, AZ 85012-2402

Arkansas
Bldg. 65, Fort Roots
2200 Fort Roots Drive
North Little Rock, AR 72114-1756

California
11000 Wilshire Boulevard
Los Angeles, CA 90024-3602

1301 Clay Street
Oakland, CA 94612-5209

8810 Rio San Diego Drive
San Diego, CA 92108-1508

Colorado
155 Van Gordon Street
Lakewood, CO 80228
(Note: Known as the Denver VA Regional Office)

Connecticut
555 Willard Avenue, Building 2E
Newington, CT 06111
(Co-located with the VACT Health Care System, Newington Campus)

Delaware
VA Medical and Regional Office Center
1601 Kirkwood Highway
Wilmington, DE 19805-4988

District of Columbia
1722 I (Eye) Street NW
Washington, DC 20421-1111

Florida
P.O. Box 1437
St. Petersburg, FL 33731-1437
(On the campus of the Bay Pines VA Medical Center)

Georgia
1700 Clairmont Road
Decatur, GA 30033-4032

Hawaii
Spark Matsunaga Medical & Regional Office Center (VAMROC)
459 Patterson Road
Honolulu, HI 96819-1522

Idaho
805 W. Franklin Street
Boise, ID 83702-5560

Illinois
2122 W. Taylor Street
Chicago, IL 60612

Indiana
575 N. Pennsylvania Street
Indianapolis, IN 46204-1526

Iowa
210 Walnut Street
Des Moines, IA 50309-9825

Kansas
VA Medical and Regional Office Center
5500 E. Kellogg
Wichita, KS 67218-1698

Kentucky
321 W. Main Street
Louisville, KY 40202-6200

Louisiana
671A Whitney Avenue
Gretna, LA 70056-2692

Maine
VA Medical and Regional Office Center
1 VA Center, Bldg. 248
Togus, ME 04330-6795

Maryland
31 Hopkins Plaza
Baltimore, MD 21201-0001

Massachusetts
John F. Kennedy Building
Government Center
Boston, MA 02203-0393

Michigan
477 Michigan Avenue
Detroit, MI 48226-2591

Minnesota
VA Regional Office and Insurance Center
1 Federal Drive Bldg., Fort Snelling
St. Paul, MN 55111-4050

Mississippi
1600 E. Woodrow Wilson Avenue
Jackson, MS 39216-5102

Missouri
400 S. 18th Street
St. Louis, MO 63103-2676

Montana
VA Medical and Regional Office Center
Williams Street, Hwy. 12 West
Fort Harrison, MT 59636-9999

Nebraska
5631 S. 48th Street
Lincoln, NE 68516-4198

Nevada
5460 Reno Corporate Drive
Reno, NV 89511

New Hampshire
275 Chestnut Street
Manchester, NH 03101-2489

New Jersey
20 Washington Place
Newark, NJ 07102-3174

New Mexico
500 Gold Avenue SW
Albuquerque, NM 87102-3118

New York
130 S. Elmwood Avenue
Buffalo, NY 14202-2478

245 W. Houston Street
New York, NY 10014-4805

North Carolina
251 N. Main Street
Winston-Salem, NC 27155-1000

North Dakota
VA Medical & Regional Office Center
2101 Elm Street
Fargo, ND 58102-2417

Ohio
1240 E. Ninth Street
Cleveland, OH 44199-2001

Oklahoma
125 S. Main Street
Muskogee, OK 74401-7025

Oregon
1220 SW 3rd Avenue
Portland, OR 97204-2825

Pennsylvania
VA Regional Office and Insurance Center
5000 Wissahickon Avenue
Philadelphia, PA 19101-8079

Pennsylvania
1000 Liberty Avenue
Pittsburgh, PA 15222-4004

Rhode Island
380 Westminster Mall
Providence, RI 02903-3246

South Carolina
1801 Assembly Street
Columbia, SC 29201-2495

South Dakota
VA Medical and Regional Office Center
2501 W. 2nd Street
Sioux Falls, SD 57117-5046

Tennessee
110 Ninth Avenue South
Nashville, TN 37203-3817

Texas
6900 Almeda Road
Houston, TX 77030-4200

One Veterans Plaza
701 Clay Avenue
Waco, TX 76799-0001

Utah
550 Foothill Drive
Salt Lake City, Utah 84113

Vermont
VA Medical and Regional Office Center
215 N. Main Street
White River Junction, VT 05009-0001

Virginia
210 Franklin Road SW
Roanoke, VA 24011-2204

Washington
915 Second Avenue
Seattle, WA 98174-1060

West Virginia
640 4th Avenue
Huntington, WV 25701-1340

Wisconsin
5400 W. National Avenue
Milwaukee, WI 53214

Wyoming
(Served by the Denver VA Regional Office)
155 Van Gordon Street
Lakewood, CO 80228

Philippines
U.S. Department of Veterans Affairs
1131 Roxas Boulevard
FPO AP 96515-1110
Manila, PI

Puerto Rico
150 Ave. Carlos Chardon, Suite 232
San Juan, PR 00936-4867

INDEX